# SELF-APPROVED

*A Guide for Authentic and Purposeful Living*

NECIE BLACK

*Self-Approved: A Guide for Authentic and Purposeful Living*
© 2017 by Necie Black

ISBN: 978-0-9984552-1-1

All rights reserved. No part of this book may be reproduced or transmitted in any form or by any means, electronic or mechanical, including photocopying and recording, or by an information storage and retrieval system, without permission in writing from the author.

Book cover designed by Crystal Manu crystal.manu1@gmail.com

# Contents

Foreword ............................................................................. 7

Introduction: From My Heart to Yours ................................. 9

Chapter 1: Self-Esteem—The Confidence Gap ..................... 13

Chapter 2: Self-Validation and Its Healing Ability ................ 27

Chapter 3: The Process of Self-Assessment ........................... 39

Chapter 4: Allow Your Gifts Their Space .............................. 53

Chapter 5: Subscribe to Self-Care Therapy ............................ 65

Chapter 6: Turn Your Vision into Action .............................. 79

Chapter 7: Build Relationships That Work ........................... 91

Chapter 8: For Every Milestone Achieved,
  Affirm and Celebrate ........................................................ 105

Chapter 9: Trust and Celebrate Your Progress ...................... 115

Epilogue: Rules of Engagement ............................................ 119

For love ♥

I am blessed beyond measure! Grateful and thankful for the presence of my Lord and Savior Jesus Christ. Thank you for loving me when I didn't love myself. Thank you, Lord, for holding my hand the many times I let go of yours. Thank you, Holy Spirit, for protecting, comforting, and nudging me along my life's journey.

To my Lyfemate and the Love of my Life—my husband Michael T. Black. There are no words to describe the honor I feel being your wife. I love you, beyond.

For my daughters, Tenesia, Naomi, Michaella and Jewell, my granddaughters, KeAna, Leah, Kaitlyn and Alyna, and all the young ladies I've had the pleasure to impart wisdom—this book is for you. Always remember the power you hold inside. Define your own standard of beauty. Celebrate the woman you are becoming. Be curious and passionate for life.

The future awaits your divine presence. Be Brilliant!

I love you!

# Foreword

Have you ever gotten financial advice from someone who owes you money or made an appointment with a new hair stylist who could really use a good conditioning treatment? It doesn't feel good and most likely you'd shy away from recommending them to family and friends based on your personal experience.

But when someone like Necie Black offers wisdom and tools needed to create a lifestyle that's in alignment with your purpose, I know that she is speaking from the heart and that her life is a reflection of the words she speaks and writes, and I'm excited about the lives her new book will impact.

Necie approaches her craft as a Life Coach, speaker and author with refreshing honesty and transparency that elicits feelings of trust, acceptance and openness from the clients and audiences she serves. She speaks from the heart as she shares stories of the fear, lack of confidence and unworthiness she once felt. Through her spiritual walk, and willingness to search for truth she has learned self-forgiveness and has made it her life's work to help women move beyond the point in their lives where they are weighed down by their troubled pasts.

Even though I know Necie's story, I did not know her before she had incorporated the mechanisms and skills that have brought her to the where she is today. But who she is now is certainly a testimony to the work she has developed and is sharing with the world.

The truth is not always easy to hear but it is always what is needed for positive change and growth.

I don't know what negative thoughts and memories from the past lurk in your mind, but as a rape survivor, I do know that finding ways to deal with trauma can save you years of sadness, insecurity and pain.

I wish Necie's book *Self-Approved* had been available to me back then, but I'm so glad that it's available to you now, in this season of your life. Today is your day. I know you will be blessed by this book as much as I have been blessed by knowing Necie as a friend and colleague. Her unwavering ability to make tough decisions with candor and fairness has earned her respect and her sense of humor always-ready to party demeanor make her a joy to be around.

I can assure you that her message of hope, self-discovery, and self-validation is right on time.

—Nikki Woods

# INTRODUCTION:
# From My Heart to Yours

Dear Daughters, Sisters and Mothers,

When I decided to write this book, I had you in mind. Why? Because I believe in many ways we are alike. I believe we have spent a greater part of our lives searching for meaning. Believing there is more, yet struggling to find a place where we belonged. I believe you're like me, because you know the meaning of hard work, dedication and sacrifice. We've done everything we can to put a painful past behind us and move forward to create a better life. Instead, we wonder if we are enough, if we're *doing* enough and when we will *have* enough. At times, we shrink at opportunities because they involve risk, believing we can't afford to make yet another mistake. You and I, we watch others do what they love, hoping one day we'll get it together and move out of the cozy comfort zone we've created, hoping one day we can loosen the grip of the mask we hold tightly to our faces, and let it fall away. That mask—oh, we've hidden behind it well. It's kept our secrets, fears and hopes well hidden from the world. Heck, we started believing we *were* the mask and that's why it's difficult to let it go. Who are we without it? Never mind. Soon we'll have the courage to expose ourselves to the world and not give a care what others think about God's masterpiece. It'll happen one day, so we wait. We wait on the wings of life to bring the strength and direction we need. The years continue to roll by, with us dreaming about life instead of getting out there and experiencing it.

My sister, I awoke to realize dreaming is not enough. I had to stand up **to** me—**for** me. I had to break the chains fear wrapped around my existence and hold myself responsible for discovering me. To forgive myself for the past and those who hurt me, I had to believe who God said I was. I had to remove the negative residue that clouded my thinking and blinded me to the truth—the truth that I really can do all things through Jesus Christ who is my strength. The truth is that I was enough—am enough—and always will be enough. I mean seriously, if God knows everything about me (past, present and future) and *still* approves of me, who am I not to approve of myself? All that I am is in Him. Everything I have is because of Him. Who I become is through Him.

As believers, we can no longer stand on excuses or hide behind a mask. There is a level of personal responsibility in making dreams a reality. Have faith in yourself and take back the power you've given to others for their approval. It is my commitment to be secure *within*, to trust who I am, and create a lifestyle of action that aligns with my purpose. I believe deep down you feel the same. If you are hoping someday, someone will give you permission to boldly step into your greatness— that *someday* is today. That *someone* is you! Join with me in this adventure and let's decree, "We will not allow anything outside of ourselves to validate us any longer." Gather the courage, make

## INTRODUCTION: FROM MY HEART TO YOURS

the decision and change your life! We will rise as awakened women and thrive in a life of authenticity, purpose and power. God has already *approved* you. Stamp **Approved** on yourself and go get your life.

Yours in the journey.

xoxo,

Necie

# CHAPTER 1:

# Self-Esteem—The Confidence Gap

*"The man who does not value himself, cannot value anything or anyone."*

—Ayn Rand

How many times have you stepped out on the skinny branch to fly, only to fall, crashing to the ground? An enormous desire to do something greater fills your heart, but you wait. Maybe you've decided your heart can't take the pain of another disappointment. Or perhaps you were abused or beaten by the hands of someone who promised to love and protect you. So now you question whether you are worth anything at all, or question why God created you in the first place. Are there voices whispering, "You will never amount to anything," and they're stuck on replay in your mind? While you applaud the accomplishments of others are you secretly jealous? The twinges of envy felt while scrolling through *success stories* on social media can make you compare their lives to yours. It's okay to be honest and admit you feel lost. Just remember, denial is what keeps you from pinpointing the exact thing holding you back and it forces you to take life's cues and direction from others. People will tell you what you should be doing and what they think is better for you. *Do this, do that, take shortcuts,* they say. It doesn't have to feel right or align with your internal nudging, but it will allow you to fit into relationships that suck the joy and peace out of you.

Does any of this sound familiar? Well, you can no longer put off facing the truth: fear is an issue. Scared out of your wits, fear stopped you from believing the promises of God and cluttered your mind with junk. Fear showed you how to take short-cuts that led to short-term and unfulfilling gain. And now, fear is eating away at two of your most valuable assets: confidence and self-esteem.

I'm not pointing fingers because I was in every one of the above-mentioned scenarios. Struggling with my identity caused me to take on the personality of others, trying to be who I wasn't. Hitching myself to people not aligned with me created an identity crisis. The louder their voices rang as truth in my head, the less important my voice became. Some days I didn't know whether I was coming or going, but didn't connect the dots between how I was feeling and low self-esteem. Interestingly, low self-esteem impacts everyone's life differently. It manifests itself through fear, frustration, doubt, perfectionism and controlling behavior. Whereas one person may isolate themselves from society when they feel inadequate and unworthy, someone else may insert themselves into society and over-compensate to fit in. Doing both makes it easy to hide inadequacies in one area of life, especially if you are successful in another, and that was me.

Let me share a bit of back story. After leaving a physically abusive marriage in the 80's, my kids and I moved back home with Mama and my stepdad. A few months before leaving my ex, I had lost the only job I had since graduating high school. With no husband or job, I spent most of the time moping around feeling sorry for myself. It was such a desperate period in life and I lost a lot of weight, from 130lbs to ending up around 110lbs. I got by with working odd jobs here and there. Rarely was the money enough to cover the few bills I had like daycare, bus fare and contributing to my parent's household when I could. The cost of daycare back then was nothing compared to what it is today, but even then, it felt like a million dollars. I was creative at combining the income from two part-time jobs to make them work as if I had full-time employment. I once had a noon to 6pm shift at a check cashing store, then I rushed home to get the kids fed and in bed before heading to an overnight job processing credit card payments. Piecing jobs together gave me time to take the kids to school, participate in job interviews, and be home in the evening before the overnight shift began.

It was exhausting most days but it was like—whatever. Surviving meant you drudge along and make the best of it. Then, one day during my job search, I saw an ad in the newspaper about the local phone company hiring for administration positions. The talk around town was the company only hired relatives, or you had to know someone on the inside. I had no relatives there and knew no one there, but decided it wouldn't hurt to try. I took a chance, caught the bus to their office and applied for one of the advertised positions. After completing the application, the lady looked it over, looked at me, and asked if I had time to take a typing test. *"Why yes, I have plenty of time,"* I said, suddenly excited. All the while I was thinking it would make me late for work. Well, there was no way I'd miss an opportunity to work at the phone company. My brain reeled with the possibility of moving into an apartment of my own and doing everything I wanted for my kids.

After passing the typing test, the lady said someone would contact me the following week. She scribbled her name and number on a piece of paper and I tucked it away next to my driver's license for safekeeping. After a week passed with no phone call, I told myself they didn't want to hire me but didn't have the decency to call. Negative thoughts clouded my mind about how I wasn't good enough to work for this company. Doubt told me I didn't deserve anything better than what I had. Finally, I decided at least I should call and know for sure—that way I could stop waiting. I remember being so afraid my hands shook as I dialed the number, hanging up a few times before anyone answered. Fear told me not to embarrass myself because I faced certain rejection. "Stop it," I yelled at myself, as I took a deep breath and dialed the number. I held the receiver to my ear until a lady answered. I gave her my name and told her why I was calling before she put me on hold. It seemed like forever, but when she returned she sounded excited. I found out she had been unable to reach me, was glad I called and offered me a job.

Thank God I called! I gladly accepted the job and started training the following Monday. I was thrilled to land a position with a large corporation and bring home full-time income and benefits. Learning new systems and processes helped me transition to different areas of the company and I fit in perfectly. You couldn't tell me I hadn't made it. I felt strong, secure and confident in my new career. I worked hard to gain the approval of everyone there. The salary was great, and I was finally able to do more for my family and finish the degree I had started years prior. Everything was going so well and I worked hard to prove

## SELF-ESTEEM—THE CONFIDENCE GAP

myself a valuable asset to the company. In the process, I thrived on the praise, pats on the back and "atta-girls" for a job well done. The louder the praise, the harder I worked. Applause was my drug of choice and it was this type of external validation to which I became addicted.

*"Most people love you for who you pretend to be. To keep their love, you keep pretending—performing."*

—Jim Morrison

I left my first marriage with very little self-esteem, doing what was necessary to survive. I was proud to be a single mama "holding it down" by society's standards. I was determined to prove I was not a failure because of past mistakes, so I shaped myself into society's mold. I had a good job, house, car and the status that came with a good job. While I was riding high professionally, I still had no idea who I was personally. At work, I could bury insecurities because I didn't have to be liked. My paycheck was based on performance: follow the rules and color inside the lines. Completing tasks, meeting deadlines and taking care of customers yielded the accolades I wanted and validated me in ways I found thrilling. Here's what the Merriam-Webster dictionary says about validation: "an act or process used to prove validity, value or worth." For validation to occur, there must be proof of value. I proved myself valuable based on the job I did, and it led to me associating my work performance with self-worth. It worked out so well in my professional career so I started "performing" in personal relationships, thinking I could keep the attention of my partner of the moment. Money. Sex. Time. Whatever it took to keep them happy, I obliged. I sacrificed my dignity to keep them interested and pretended to be who I thought they wanted. Doing so led me to another dysfunctional marriage.

Honestly, I reveled in book smarts, not so much in the street smarts department or sensing when I was being used. I didn't know how to judge character, and blindly trusted my heart to those who didn't deserve it. I chose my partner's happiness over my own, thinking if I gave them what they wanted I'd get what I needed in return. What I needed was to feel loved, appreciated and valued for who I was, not who I pretended to be. Suppressed anger and resentment drained every ounce of self-esteem I had. Exhausted trying to maintain a façade, I no longer had the strength to battle the demons privately.

In yet another marriage on the verge of failure, questioning my ability to have good relationships took its toll on my confidence. What's worse, this one acted as if he were doing me a favor by being married to me. I long overstayed my welcome that time, but found it difficult to just let go. Maybe because this marriage wasn't physically abusive like the first one, I believed it could work out if I just…. submit and obey. I couldn't see how the emotional stress was draining me just as badly as physical stress. There were times when all I wanted to do was sleep, so I checked out and didn't have to face the problems. We eventually separated. After many nights of crying into my pillow, I decided that if change was coming, I needed to do something different. Don't you get tired of crying? Tired of being sick and tired and getting nowhere?

I began to look at myself closely, spent time in scripture and gained a bit of confidence, just enough to take a bold stand about the marriage. Honestly, I didn't want the marriage anymore, but since I'd been divorced once already, being alone felt daunting. Fear offered me justification for mediocrity. Fear fed my ego with a false sense of love. Afraid to be judged for a second failed marriage, I had to call it like it was and confront all that made me fearful. And you know what's odd? I wasn't afraid of being alone physically; that was an excuse. I was married and felt alone. The real issue was I was afraid of being myself. I was comfortable hiding behind the mask; scared that if I peeked out, there would be no one there to validate me. Afraid that no one would accept the real me. How had I missed that? Didn't I believe in the law of reciprocity? You know, treat others the way you wanted to be treated? That's what I tried to do, except not everyone operates the same, and I feared rejection even after everything I was learning about me. What a bold realization and an extremely scary place.

All the time I spent in church, I had been reading scriptures, praying and pouring my heart out to God and waiting on him to fix it. How could I still be stuck needing the approval of others to confirm or deny what I thought about myself? Was I just going through the motions? How could I confess Christ and not see myself through His eyes? Yes, this was a bold and scary place indeed. I struggled as if there was no hope.

Then truth came for me and I had to answer. It was the revelation of things I didn't pray on because I was afraid of the truth. Have you ever avoided a conversation with God because you already knew the answer? You pray *around* the issue and say to yourself, "God knows my heart." Fact was I held on to what was easy and comfortable. Change was hard and facing the truth was painful. I knew at that moment it was my responsibility to validate myself, to give myself what I expected others to give me.

I gathered some resolve, a bit of dignity and walked away from the marriage in 2001. When I did, there was an expectation of internal peace and promise in my heart, a reassurance that life would be better and I would never be the same.

I slowly revealed the woman behind the mask and resisted the urges to apologize for being me. Removing the mask strengthened my self-esteem and built the confidence and courage I needed to bring normalcy to my life. Drama and chaos were no longer welcome in my life or home. I became comfortable with what I wanted and embraced what was genuinely true and unique about me. Authenticity brought a realization of the difference between living as if I'm happy versus being happy while living. The difference is believing what God says about you and trusting who you are through His eyes. Being honest with myself was one of the toughest things to do, yet it was very necessary to keep me from picking up another mask. Love me. Hate me. It doesn't matter. Self-respect became a priority and ushered in a thirst to live an authentic life.

## Self-Esteem, Confidence and Validation

Self-esteem is love, respect and belief in yourself. It is the ability to admire the person you are, the talent you possess and the value you bring. A lot of how you feel about yourself comes from experiences growing up and the results of what you do to make your own mark on the world. You think you are successful when you do something that generates a good result. The same holds true when you do something that fails, and you feel like a failure. Failure and success are similar, in that both are the result of an action taken. Just because an action doesn't yield the result you want, that doesn't mean you personally are a failure. It

## SELF-ESTEEM—THE CONFIDENCE GAP

means the action failed. The goal is not to attach your self-worth to the outcome of an action. What happens when you've done everything right and the outcome isn't what you want? Well, it depends on your ability to separate the outcome from self-value, tweak the action and not be afraid to push forward. It's normal to have some level of trepidation after a setback; just remember to keep fear in its place and call it out for what it is—a confidence killer. Think about a situation where you did everything the right way and didn't get the result you wanted. Remember the circumstances and how you felt during the moment. What was the outcome's impact to your confidence?

_____

_____

_____

_____

_____

If what you *do* fails, don't take it personally as if *you've* failed. Detaching self-worth from the action is what keeps you grounded and unshaken by the ups and downs of life's challenges. Positive self-esteem fills the gap between insecurity and confidence, and positivity *is* something to take personally.

Processing information in a different way boosts self-esteem and closes the confidence gap. Instead of viewing past struggles as failures, consider them learning opportunities that are necessary to making better choices. For instance, I learned what I wanted in a good relationship by having experienced bad ones. My life is flourishing in marriage now because it's based on the mutual love and respect that began within me. Coming to terms with the past allows you to be in a place not just to love yourself, but to be genuine and open to accept true love when it comes. In turn, you can allow others to be themselves as well.

## The Need for Approval

> *"I prefer to be true to myself, even at the hazard of incurring the ridicule of others, rather than to be false, and to incur my own abhorrence."*
>
> —Frederick Douglass

Most people aren't high in confidence even when they appear to be. There is conflict with your inner critic, the small nagging voice in your head that says you're not good, strong or smart enough. Even when you have proven successes, there's still an element of trepidation when doing something new or different. Sometimes just encountering people who look and think differently creates anxiety about proper etiquette. Here are a few situations where low self-esteem may have shown up for you:

- Staying in a position where you are no longer happy.
- Waiting for permission to live the way you want.
- Not speaking up when your opinion is necessary.
- Hesitation in asking for a desired and deserved raise.
- Believing the cute guy is out of your league.
- Measuring yourself against the success of others.
- Spending money on things you don't need to make yourself feel better.

## SELF-ESTEEM—THE CONFIDENCE GAP

- Not feeling worthy of a compliment extended.
- Wanting someone to rescue you from a problem or situation.

Now you might think those who lack confidence will continue to suffer disadvantages, but it's not at all true. Internal conflict can have a stronghold of momentary doubt on just about everyone at some point in life. It's important not to dwell in doubt or allow thoughts of inadequacy to prevent you from doing what you want or need to do. Trust yourself and apply for the job. Ask for the raise. Make the phone call. Wave away the cloud of doubt; step out and be in action. You won't know what you can or can't do until you start, right? Sure, there is pain in growth and growing stronger. But if you stand your ground, you can make it through the transitional period of discomfort. Don't try to be perfect. Perfectionism is overrated and lacks flexibility as it relates to growth. Give yourself the grace and space to err. Too many women are afraid to fail, to make a mistake—to take a chance. Everything in life has a cost wrapped up in the fine print, and it's not always money. Cost can be a sacrifice of time, energy, resources and the temporary stretching of your faith. But I counter that by asking you: What is fear and complacency costing you? A promotion? Opportunity? A good relationship? Peace of mind and self-respect?

I encourage you to push through negative self-perceptions. Your mind is the most powerful weapon against defeat, poverty, brokenness, adversity and low self-esteem. Healing for your heart begins with your thoughts. How? Your mind determines how you see yourself, what you focus on and what you speak over your life. Stop thinking you can't make it, or that you don't have what it takes to (fill in the blank). Yes, evict negative thoughts and replace them with powerful and positive ones. If you want to shift the direction of your life, you must think first, then speak in the direction you want to go. In moments of doubt, talk to yourself in the same way you would a girlfriend who was feeling less than confident. You are already prepared for the next level in your life, career and relationship. Release others from the responsibility of validating you, because their validation only provides temporary confidence. You must be able to stand when no one applauds. Validating and esteeming yourself from within is lasting and much more powerful. Go ahead and make your mark. You are already God approved.

## Recap and Challenge

It's no secret that fear is the culprit behind low self-esteem. Fear of not being accepted, not being adequate, not being, doing or having enough. Because of fear, many people spend time settling for less than they deserve. Time. It's a commodity that once spent you will never have again. There will not be another moment just like the one you are experiencing right now. Life is full of disappointment and struggle, no matter what you do. You will win some, lose some and sometimes you will break even. Show up anyway. It doesn't matter what didn't work out or who doesn't approve of you. Spend no more precious time fixated on what you don't have, and commit to everything you do.

- Be who you are. There is no need to fake or pretend you are someone or something you're not.
- Self-validation comes from within. Resist becoming dependent on the praise and approval of others.

## SELF-ESTEEM—THE CONFIDENCE GAP

- Admire the person you are, and believe in your unique combination of talent, experiences and capabilities.
- Don't allow success or failure to define your self-worth. When challenges arise, allow yourself the grace to adjust and continue to move forward.

Remember earlier in the chapter, I asked you to think about a situation where you did everything you were supposed to do and things didn't work out. What was your response to that question? If you didn't answer it, go back and think about the impact the situation had on your confidence. Perhaps it gave you motivation to try harder, or it made you frustrated to the point of quitting. I challenge you to identify **one** thing you will do differently to move forward. Dare to imagine your life on the other side of fear. Don't you agree it's time to start being, doing and having beyond what you've settled for? Give yourself permission to start over. To explore possibilities, take your rightful place in the world, and make the kind of impact you desire.

SELF-APPROVED

*Notes*

CHAPTER 2:

# Self-Validation and Its Healing Ability

*"An unexpected source of confidence: individuality."*
—Dove™ #SelfEsteemProject

I fell head over heels in love with Dove™ and their mission to promote inner beauty and increase self-esteem in girls. Over the past 10 years, their movement has reached over 17 million young people with education to help them feel good about themselves. Using body confidence, this mission is helping young ladies build a positive relationship with self, as an individual, and becoming secure within to reach their full potential. Dove™ gets it by providing toolkits, resources, and social awareness to uproot poor self-esteem where it usually starts, in childhood. This type of work is especially important because seeds of insecurity are planted early in life eventually become full-grown weeds if not addressed. Those deeply embedded roots are weaved in between experiences at the most critical developmental stages of life. By the time a child reaches adulthood, insecurities are much more difficult to separate from identity.

## SELF-APPROVED

The earliest years of my life were filled with people who spoiled me. We lived in Los Angeles, down the street from family who were a constant source of love and fun for my siblings and me. We were never far away from a loving environment; my grandma was always ready with the best hugs and fresh baked goodies. Even when I was in trouble, I don't remember getting anything more than a swat on the butt that hurt my feelings more than my backside. Crying got me special attention and extra cuddles afterwards, so I was good. Mama and Daddy argued a lot, and as the arguments became more frequent, the dynamics of our lifestyle changed. My parents separated when I was seven and Mama moved us from Los Angeles to the projects of West Dallas, Texas. I was a daddy's girl, and it broke my heart to leave him behind.

In Texas, we faced a world of new people and rules. The schools were different and somewhat basic, and I skipped a grade. My teachers loved me; classmates, not so much. A few mentioned they didn't appreciate my smartness and I was picked on for being a teacher's pet. I didn't care. I was supposed to be smart with good grades. I did what the teacher said, followed the rules and was super-proud of myself. When a classmate made comments about my body, color of my skin, hair, clothes, lips, and the way I talked, I took it personally. Wanting to make friends, I spent a lot of time answering questions about where I came from. West coast dialect was a little different, and it was challenging to mimic a southern drawl. Even my skin color was too light to fit in with the darker-skinned girls, and too dark to fit in with the lighter-skinned girls. Still I was rewarded for being a good kid, selected to be a hall monitor and welcomed to join the drill team every year of grade school. I remember the hot pink and black crushed velvet uniform my grandmother made for me. She sewed all my uniforms and made me feel pretty and special. It was such a happy time for me.

The sixth-grade brought a new school with different classmates. Old friends moved away and new friends were harder to make. No longer popular, I sat in the back of the classroom, kept to my studies and didn't participate in school activities. Home life changed as well, when an uncle, who moved his family in with us, began molesting me when I was ten years old. I wrote about this devastating period in my life in a chapter entitled, "When Your Truth Heals; The Necessity of Self-discovery," published in Aprille Franks-Hunt's anthology *Fabulous New Life*. I shared how the molestation progressed over the years from touching at age ten to rape when I was thirteen. *"I was filled with fear and uncertainty, and it broke my spirit, my faith, my confidence and my self-esteem as I attempted to bury the memory and continue with life."* My mind told me to stay quiet and not tell anyone. *Don't think about it and please God don't let it happen again.* Imagine a child trying to understand the betrayal of someone who said they would love and protect them. There is no understanding. I share this because I want you to see how one event in your life can change how you see yourself from that moment on. It is where low self-esteem and body shame began for me, just as something equally as devastating did for many other young women. My body became a source of shame, and I faded into the background of life. Awkward and uncomfortable in my skin, I tried desperately not to be noticed; not for being smart, not for being pretty—not at all.

There was a ray of hope when I became a freshman in high school. I started a new school where I knew no one, and hoped it would be better than middle school. I didn't want to hide anymore and wanted to feel special again, like I did in grade school. I wanted to be involved again, so took a chance and joined the pep club as a prerequisite to becoming a cheerleader. That freshman year was a blast, bringing normalcy and a sense of belonging back to my life. I laughed a lot, made a ton of friends, and loved the excitement of dancing and cheering at football games. I tried out for cheerleader at the end of my freshman year and made the squad. Honestly, I didn't see myself fitting the mold of how cheerleaders were expected to look. I wasn't as flexible as everyone else. My jumps were not as high and my knocked knees got in the way sometimes. I envied the talent of those in leadership and bent over backwards to prove I was good enough. I practiced at home well after dark to get the routine right. What I didn't understand is how low my self-esteem was. It was me who didn't think I was good enough, and I used cheering to keep me occupied so I could hide from memories. When I didn't feel beautiful, the uniform was a perfect disguise. Have you ever been in a place where you smiled and pushed through sad thoughts to show up anyhow, despite how you felt? I was going to fit in, no matter what. No one needed to know the shame, and putting on a mask brought my conformity to the rules of the crowd.

I learned a valuable lesson about people. Some will demean you to make themselves feel better. One day I was having a "not-so-beautiful moment," and I messed up on stage at a pep rally. I tried to shake it off, when a female classmate said to me, "Wow, your lips are big, and why are they so wrinkly?"

I subconsciously licked my lips and stared at her, saying nothing. She walked away with a smirk, leaving me feeling worse. Was this intentional? Was she trying to hurt my feelings?

The moment stayed in my mind until another female classmate asked, "What color gloss are you wearing?" Uh oh! My stomach became queasy and I defensively asked why. "Cause your lips are gorgeous," she said.

I wasn't expecting a compliment, and slowly cracked a smile. Still feeling a bit self-conscious, I asked if she thought my lips were too big.

She replied, "Nah, why would I think that?"

I told her I thought they were, too ashamed to admit someone else's opinion was why I asked. I breathed a sigh of relief when she didn't press the issue. I left school feeling a bit better. Beauty really is in the eye of the beholder. I'd heard that phrase many times and it clicked in the moment. Suddenly, I didn't feel the need to work so hard to impress other classmates because some liked me, some didn't, and I distanced myself from those who attempted to make me feel small.

Appearances can be deceiving. Self-degradation is a serious issue for women of all ages. Not everyone who smiles is happy on the inside. The truth is that you aren't born with low self-esteem; it comes because of your attitude towards negative situations. Attitude is a little word that makes a big difference in how you feel about you, the world around you, and how you see yourself. There are women who can't look themselves in the mirror because they are ashamed of their bodies or don't feel worthy to call themselves beautiful. Maybe they were criticized, made fun of, molested or rejected, and now self-loathing thoughts run rampant in their minds. It doesn't matter how the seeds of lack were planted; they can be uprooted with awareness and intentional action.

**External validation** is a game of compliments to provide approval based on performance or physical appearance. Sure, it's human nature to want to be around people who make you feel good and appreciate your contribution. So yes, being validated by others is a good thing. What's not good is growing dependent on the applause of others to feel good. What's not good is sacrificing who you are for the sake of being liked or accepted. Think about it. What happens if the compliments stop? When the applause slows, do you feel unappreciated or dismissed? Realistically, you'll have days where you are on top of the world. You are confident, making connections and feeling supported. Other days, you feel as if no one has time for you, as your calls and texts go unanswered. Does it mean you stop being amazing? Not at all. This space is a moment for self-reliance and validation. Gain the confidence to get out there, find your own answers and be your own cheerleader.

Having an air of confidence is important in situations such as a job interviews, where they judge both your skills and how you carry yourself. There are times when you are extremely qualified but lack confidence, and it can make the difference between breaking or sealing the deal. In fact, lack of confidence is high on the chart (along with discrimination) as one of the reasons men are paid more than women in the workplace. Imagine working the same position and hours, with the same results, and receiving pay that is less than your male counterpart. Yet per the Department of Labor Bureau of Labor Statistics, women earned 83 cents for every $1 a man earns; 83%, and this discrepancy varies with occupation. Even in jobs such as education, healthcare support and personal care services, where women are the majority, men still earn more. How can that be? I believe lack of confidence and self-esteem is part of the problem and here's why.

A study published in the Journal of Personality and Social Psychology in 2015 indicates there's still a confidence gender gap among women in Western countries. *"During the past two decades, a large number of studies on age and gender differences in self-esteem have found that men have higher self-esteem than women and that both men and women show age-graded increases in self-esteem."* said Wiebke Bleidorn, PhD. *"This is likely the result of specific cultural influences that guide self-esteem development in men and women."*[1] Women can close this gap by taking the initiative to know and trust themselves in a deeper, more intimate way.

The confidence gap in our country comes from a culture that limits the potential of women, beginning in their childhood. Society decides what careers are suitable for women, so little girls are steered in that direction. While women are gaining significant ground by stepping outside of stereotypical roles for more influential ones, there is still work to do. Too many spend time doubting, warring over following their hearts vs. settling within society's limits.

Ladies, we aren't exercising faith in self or being assertive enough in asking for raises, promotions and positions that align with our skillsets. Remove limiting thoughts that don't serve

---

1 "Age and Gender Differences in Self-Esteem—A Cross-Cultural Window," by Wiebke Bleidorn, PhD, University of California, Davis, and Tilburg University; Ruben Arslan, MSc, Georg-August-Universität Göttingen; Jaap Denissen, PhD, Tilburg University; Peter Rentfrow, PhD, University of Cambridge; Jochen Gebauer, PhD, University of Mannheim; and Jeff Potter, BSc, Atof Inc., *Journal of Personality and Social Psychology*, published online Dec. 21, 2015.

you and know you are worthy of having all you desire. If there is anything *you* have told yourself, or someone else has told you that has created doubt, now's the time to uproot it. There is nothing you can't achieve when you rely on validation from within and when you resist the stigmas placed on you by others.

But how? The first step is to adjust your attitude. See your beauty without society's idea of "perfect." With social media, women are flooded with marketing campaigns and quick-fix advertising. Our preoccupation with beauty, class, style and status has created a saturation of companies focused on monetizing your insecurities. I don't know of anyone who hasn't wished for a summer beach body or created New Year's resolutions that don't last beyond March. I can't count how many times I slathered my body with gels, mud or cream concoctions and wrapped myself in plastic, hoping to drop ten pounds in ten minutes. Once I spent $99.00 on a thigh thingy that promised to strengthen and tone my inner thighs. What I didn't know was I could get the same results with a pair of resistance bands for $5.00 because I still had to do the work.

Like me, if you're not careful, you'll waste unnecessary time and money on empty promises that leave you feeling as if something is wrong with you, when there isn't. Does this mean you shouldn't build a stronger body or accentuate your natural beauty with makeup and special treatments? Not at all. Even if you opt for body adjustments like surgery, it's your body and your choice. Do it for you, not to gain the approval of anyone else or to adhere to a societal standard. The shape of your legs, curves of your hips, and the angles of your face make you uniquely different. Imagine how boring life would be if there wasn't something special to set you apart from someone else.

Physical appearance will never replace inner beauty—with or without surgery.

Holding your head up and standing tall, with shoulders square and back straight, gives you a feeling of health and confidence, even when you don't feel confident. Your body language and posture affects the thoughts you have about yourself and quite possibly the ability to perform. At Ohio State University, 71 students participated in a two-part experiment studying body posture.[2] One part tested whether body posture affects confidence. *"The results show how our body posture can affect not only what others think about us, but also how we think about ourselves,"* said Richard Petty, co-author of the study and professor of psychology at Ohio State University.

The way you carry yourself and how you interact with others are important opportunities to exhibit self-confidence, when you might feel it the least. Be aware of how your body language speaks, and follow these tips for improving posture. Practice first by standing with your back against a wall: shoulders straight, chin lifted slightly and eyes slightly smiling. If you're sitting, scoot your hips to the back of the chair so your upper back, shoulders and hips are against the back of the chair and your back is straight. Put your feet flat on the floor in front of you and hold the position for several minutes at a time. To help build confidence when you don't really feel it, try these additional tips:

1. When speaking, make eye contact with others and smile naturally. This shows you are warm, inviting and comfortable with yourself.

---

2 Briñol, P., Petty, R. E. and Wagner, B. (2009), Body posture effects on self-evaluation: A self-validation approach. *Eur. J. Soc. Psychol.*, 39: 1053–1064. doi:10.1002/ejsp.607

2. Speak clearly and loudly enough to be heard. Resist speaking in a low tone unless you're in a quiet setting. Even then, make sure to enunciate and don't slur or mumble your words.
3. Confident people don't need to be the center of attention all the time, and they don't feel the need to have their egos stroked. Just relax and enjoy meeting new people.
4. Never be afraid to admit you don't know. Be inquisitive and explore answers; you will learn something new and build confidence through knowledge.

As you begin to find within yourself what you had expected others to give you, explore every step of discovery. Allow self-validation to heal each broken place you've been band-aiding all these years. You are valuable beyond measure. There is now and never will be anyone just like you, and that alone is worth giving yourself a high-five.

## Recap and Challenge

To give yourself permission to be who you genuinely are is what self-validation does, and it boosts your confidence towards purposeful living. You don't need anyone to say it's okay for you to dream or define your own standard of beauty. Any time you feel the urge to ask others what they think of you, stop. Imagine what you want them to say and tell it to yourself. If you want to hear someone say you're beautiful, then say to yourself, "I Am Beautiful!" I challenge you to spend time getting to know your body—well. Doing so helps you recognize any changes that has taken place, not just for vanity sake, but health purposes as well.

## SELF-VALIDATION AND ITS HEALING ABILITY

Yes, it means you will stand butt naked in the mirror with a bottle of lotion or jar of cocoa butter, ready to explore your body for a few of these things:

- Look at every scar, stretch mark, dimple, mole and freckle. Check for anything that looks unusual. Was that mole there the last time you examined your body?

- Feel your curves, the shape of your breasts and the spine in your back. Does anything feel out of proportion? What about lumps, knots or sore spots?

- How does your skin look and feel? Healthy skin has a natural glow. With plenty of water, you nourish from the inside out. From the outside, go ahead and slather on the lotion or cocoa butter to help keep your skin soft and supple.

Make sure to talk to your doctor about anything out of the ordinary. The more you learn about your body, the easier it is to recognize potential health threats. As you grow comfortable with your naked glory, the less critical you will feel towards it. That-a-Girl! Love and appreciate the skin you are in. Dress yourself up and hold your head high. Like Mary J. says, *"Get your runway stride honed and keep it going."* Every time you pass a mirror throw yourself a kiss, smile and say how cute you look in that outfit. Wrap your arms around your whole self, flaws and all, and let your internal validation birth confidence. Confidence brings out the best **you**. Work it!

SELF-APPROVED

## CHAPTER 3:

# The Process of Self-Assessment

*"Everything that happens to you is a reflection of what you believe about yourself. We cannot outperform our level of self-esteem. We cannot draw to ourselves more than we think we are worth."*

—Iyanla Vanzant

I love this quote. It speaks directly to my heart about what it means to have a belief system that affirms who you are, why you are here and the value you bring to the world. If you have not spent time affirming what you believe to be true about yourself, you will measure everything you do against the success of others. You may set goals, create plans and jot ideas on your vision board, yet if you don't believe you can attain them, you've become the roadblock to your success. I believe what Proverbs 23:7 says when it begins, *"For as he thinketh in his heart, so is he."* This means success is only limited by what you believe in your heart is possible. Many times, your beliefs are reflections of the environment you grew up in or the people who came in and out of your life. Some who loved and protected you and others who did not. You could have restraints placed on your thinking that manipulates you into serving the purpose of others. Or maybe you have had negative experiences that left a lasting effect on your emotions and perspective. There comes a point in life when you must face the past so it does not continue to rob your future. Truth will come for you, and you must answer.

My truth came when my second marriage started to break down in 2001. Frustrated and at my wits end, I was circling inside a Christian bookstore down the street from where I lived in Plano, Texas, just looking for a little inspiration. The marriage was miserable and weighed me down with both, "I should have accomplished _____ by now" syndrome, and its partner, a case of the, "Why me, Lord?" I picked up a nice journal to record my thoughts and continued to stroll down the audio aisle. That's when I saw it: a 3-part cassette series by Bishop T.D. Jakes. Yes, I said cassette, those little square things with magnetic tape in them used to record voice and music.

I picked up the box, read the title and thought, "Oh, he's the preacher I heard about." One of my sisters had told me about the pastor of The Potter's House Church, but her only reference was all the cute men and athletes who were members. She didn't reference the preaching, teaching or how God blessed her through the service. She kept suggesting I go to church with her but I told her, "Oh no, I've got enough issues." I wanted no part of a church that only catered to the rich and well-connected. I quickly dismissed the thought of buying the cassettes, placed the package back on the shelf and walked away. Needless to say, I went around that store, up and down that same aisle I don't know how many times, but kept coming back to those cassettes. The last time I stopped, I noticed a sales tag on it. I don't remember the price, but it was some ridiculously low amount.

## THE PROCESS OF SELF-ASSESSMENT

In hindsight, God knew exactly what He was doing—setting me up with what He knew I couldn't resist—a sale. I mean, who can refuse a sale, right? Do you see how well God knows me? He gave me exactly what I needed, right when I needed it.

"Forever the Victim; I Don't Think So" was the name of the series. I began listening to the first cassettes over the next couple of days and they angered me. Who did this dude think he was, anyway, judging me the way he did, as if his sermon was speaking directly to me? I came up with every excuse in the book to counter what Bishop Jakes was preaching. "I was young and dumb, nobody told me and I trusted people too much," were my go to excuses. Still, I listened to the two remaining cassettes, despite my defense mechanisms being on high alert! He talked about being hooked on pain, stuck in a rut, and lost in the wilderness between suffering and consolation, having become a slave to the past. He spoke of having a victim mentality that causes people to live in a cycle of self-inflicted abuse, repeating the same bad choices and attracting the same type of negative people who shared their victimized mindset.

Even though I began to see myself in his sermons and how I perpetuated my own problems, I felt exposed and uncomfortable. I did **not** have the capacity to have my emotions stressed any further, so after a week or so, I slid the cassettes in the glove box of my car. After a few days of feeling an urge to listen again, I pulled the cassettes out and replayed each one over and over. Each time there was a new revelation. Oh yes, God was dealing with me through those sermons, and I did not like it one bit. Surely, I was a better person than that because, of course, I was smart. I had a degree, my own house, a good job and my kids turned out okay. My heart softened to the fact that I was responsible, at least in part, for the situations in which I found myself. Things I said I would never do, I did. Tolerating physical and mental abuse, debt, promiscuity, lies, abortions, bankruptcy—and those were the things I remembered.

Tears began pouring out of me and I could barely see the road ahead. I wiped my face with the palm of my hand. Oh God! I couldn't believe that's *exactly* me! "He's talking about me," my mind repeated with every word Bishop Jakes spoke. My heart hurt, my head hurt and I couldn't even contain the outbursts of prayers. I sobbed heavily and my chest was so tight I could hardly breathe. My mind tried desperately to keep it together, but my heart betrayed me with every beat. It felt like I was having an anxiety attack! *Oh, God, I've got to pull over.* Looking up at the rear-view mirror I was suddenly aware of the long line of cars behind me. "I'm sorry, I'm sorry," I repeated, as I signaled to get in the right-hand lane. I was barely hitting 30mph, and I slowly pulled into an empty parking lot and threw the car into park. "Dang it," I said, as I looked at the clock. 6:55 a.m. "I'll be late for work." I hit stop on the cassette player and just sat there.

Truth had come for me. Alone in the car with frazzled thoughts, a convicted heart and God. I looked at the woman I had become. The situations, circumstances, moments of my life were playing vividly in my mind, one after another. Thoughts of failure and inadequacies lined up one by one, as if to say, *"When you did this, that happened, and because you went that way, you missed this. Because you allowed this, that came, and when you rejected that, this entered the scene."* I felt hopeless, so useless. *"Look at **all** the mistakes I've made."* Then, as if in response to my thoughts, my heart said, *"Well what about this, and this, and that, and those moments? Remember when you opened your home here,*

## THE PROCESS OF SELF-ASSESSMENT

*and what about the sacrifice you made there? You didn't complain when you were asked to….and you gave your last money for that,"* as my heart attempted to prove I was still valuable. Mistakes aren't failure. I inhaled deeply and slowly released the tension. *"No matter, I'm still here. I must be here for a reason. Can't go back and change anything now,"* and a ton of other clichés crossed my mind. I beat myself up for years about the choices I had made and believed any suffering was the consequence I had to pay. I had lots of work to do, but what work exactly, I had no clue. How exactly was I supposed to attract the life I really wanted? My inner voice spoke and said, *"Take one thing at a time."* In that moment, I felt a significant growth spurt in my maturity and decided it was time to stop making excuses, be a grown-up and account for my life, its direction and decisions.

*"Your life does not get better by chance, it gets better by change."*

—Jim Rohn

Accountability begins with the process of self-assessment. Who are you? Who are you *really*, at the end of the day when you're staring at yourself in the mirror? Who have you become? Most importantly, how is that person different from the person you want to be? What's in you that pushes your inquisitive mind about what's next, believing that God gives you the desires of your heart? Answering these questions requires an examination. Just like going to the doctor for a health check, dental screening, or mammogram gives you a physical state of health report, assessment digs deeper into your emotional and mental well-being.

Find a quiet place away from the influence of others. Be intentionally selfish by shutting down thoughts that distract your honest self-reflection. Don't think about family, friends, job, church, bills, or other obligations; these moments are about you and the beginning of focus. See *you*. Not the you that you show people, but the you in this quiet moment. This space is meant to spark the thought process of personality and character issues, fears, successes, abilities and everything that shapes who you are.

To be honest, it's not always easy to improve yourself through trial and error. Make a few changes, check the results and then make a few more. If you intentionally review the actions you take through the lens of growth, you'll discover that even small tweaks in thought or behavior patterns can yield huge results. As you go deeper into self-assessment, there are three stages of focus: self-awareness, management and improvement. I call this *ICMe3™ Principles of Self-assessment* which means, "I See Me. I *see* into me, the innermost workings of my being. I am learning who I am and how to manage and improve my thoughts and behaviors." Guide yourself through this process without judgment or beating yourself up for past decisions. This is a perfect time for reflection, counting blessings and reconciliation.

1. **Self-awareness** is gaining an understanding of who you are and what's going on with you; becoming aware of what motivates you, and seeing how specific tendencies, habits and triggers are showing up in your life. It's an opportunity to view whether old negative emotions or experiences are influencing your behavior, and to see what emotional residue may exist in your heart.

## THE PROCESS OF SELF-ASSESSMENT

Emotional residue is lingering anger and frustration towards situations or people from the past that evoke emotions which no longer serve you or your plans for living. Residue happens when there is no closure and the mind and heart don't know what to do with the pain. It takes work to do something contrary to what you've been conditioned to do, but as you progress, the stronger your resolve becomes. The more you explore your emotions, the more you'll learn to understand why you feel, think, and behave the way you do, without judgment. Awareness offers a choice that lessens the chance of you sabotaging your success in life, your career and your relationships.

As part of self-awareness, think about what makes you happy, sad, afraid, angry, frustrated, excited and/or self-conscious. How do you see yourself happier, healthier and exactly where you want to be? The focus of this questioning is to take inventory of your skills, gifts, thoughts, behaviors, insecurities, and flaws (yes, those too) and review the preconceived ideas you hold about them. Negative feelings about your qualities can wreak havoc on your self-esteem. Sometimes an adjustment in perspective is necessary to allow positive thoughts to take priority. Consider the range of emotions you felt today alone. Can you remember *why* you felt the way you did? What was your trigger? Did you automatically smile at happy thoughts or are you still fuming about the person who cut you off in traffic? Be open to creating a paradigm shift in your thinking and proceed through the self-assessment. Take inventory of what you want and your emotional state. Be honest about your motives; knowing *why* something is important to you is key in establishing the time and resources to get it done.

- How do you feel about yourself, overall?
- What emotions do you feel most often?
- What do you think about where you are now?
- What do you really want?

Notice for the last question you're focusing on what you **want**, not what you don't. I recommend for this question you write at least 25 responses because most people start with generic items like, "I want to be happy," or "I want to be successful." Define happiness. Define success. Go deeper with what it looks like to you. It's okay to write whatever comes to mind first. By the time you reach numbers ten to fifteen you will have weeded out the fluff and found the meat of what's important to you. Instead of saying, "I want to be successful," define what it looks like. Is success something tangible like owning your home or car, or an intangible goal such as an ideal healthy weight? Delve deeper. Allow your mind the freedom to explore your desires beyond vague and generic goals. Because this portion of self-assessment can be a tender and vulnerable space, strengthen your resolve and push through the discomfort as you gain perspective. Only you can search your heart for answers. Imagine how much you can achieve when you're looking at yourself through the eyes of clarity and certainty. Review the list and prioritize by order of importance, with one being the most important. Keep it handy and we'll discuss creating your action plan in a later chapter.

# THE PROCESS OF SELF-ASSESSMENT

2. **Self-control** is the ability to manage your thoughts, emotions and behaviors. They are necessary internal instincts that spark action, dictate your behavior and are not always easy to control. Remember the adage, "fight or flight," coined by Walter Cannon? It suggests that when faced with a potential threat, your physiological impulse is to either run or fight. In that moment, you decide the best course of action. Fight or flight doesn't necessarily mean you're in extreme danger; it means something is forcing you to react. I've been in positions where, although angry, I chose to walk away. Just because I felt anger, it didn't mean I had to respond with anger. You have no control over the behavior of others, yet you have absolute control over your own. Take deliberate action to manage yourself by practicing what you learned through the awareness process. Make a list of habits you want to change. Include behaviors and negative self-talk that have kept you stuck in unhealthy situations and prevent you from progressing. Here are a few things to practice as you learn to control your behavior:

- When faced with a decision, pause and gather your thoughts. Visualize your desired outcome, then choose a course of action that aligns with it. Pausing allows space to weigh your options and be confident in your choices.

- Meditation and prayer work well to separate yourself from everyday noise. They can keep you calm, centered and focused, even in difficult situations.

Lean on your faith and allow it to support you in rising above challenges.

- Managing your thoughts is just as important as managing your behavior. Don't dwell on negativity. Replace negative thoughts with positive ones as soon as the negative thought enters your mind, and resist allowing cynical chatter to dominate your space.

How well you're able to self-manage is an indicator of your maturity and commitment to emotional stability. As your thought patterns and habits improve, you will grow comfortable and confident in your ability to pursue any goal you desire.

3. **Self-improvement** is necessary for consistent growth mentally, emotionally and spiritually. If you are wondering what you can do differently to improve your circumstances and bring synergy to your life, start with getting comfortable with being uncomfortable. Growth is stretching and sometimes growing will reveal things you might not want to think about, let alone do something about. Get over thinking that you are perfect, that you've got everything under control, and that you have no areas that need improving. Go ahead and say it: "I'm Not Perfect! I don't have it all together, and I'm okay." And you *are* okay! Accept the opportunity to make yourself even better. It helps to voice record or write your ideas so you can see and visualize your responses. Start by asking yourself a few questions:

    - Where are you talented and what are you good at doing? Think about the knowledge and skillset you

## THE PROCESS OF SELF-ASSESSMENT

possess. How can you create greater functionality and impact? Can you gain additional skills to complement what you already have?

- What do you enjoy doing? Think about what comes easily and brings you satisfaction. What is it about these activities that you enjoy and how can you expand on them to take them to a higher level?
- What are you afraid of? It's wise to know what gives you pause or creates moments of doubt. The more you intentionally face fear, the less power it will hold over you.
- What areas need improvement? Perhaps it's your attitude, personality, communication or soft skills in dealing with others. Don't make excuses or blame others for how you view life. If necessary, ask someone you trust for their honest feedback.

Reading books and taking classes are a great start for expanding your mind. You might also consider including new life experiences in your self-improvement journey. I challenge you to travel to new places and meet new people. Network and interact with others who don't look, think or act like you to broaden your perspective. Release the creativity in you and birth new ideas. Surround yourself with people who force you to move out of your comfort zone, those who challenge your thinking and present alternatives for you to consider. Limited exposure equals limited perspective, so explore beyond what's familiar. Create a paradigm shift by expanding your skillset, deepen your knowledge and position yourself as a woman of authenticity and influence.

## Recap and Challenge

Self-assessment allows you to review yourself from a place of improvement, never judgment. Openness to the aspects of your behaviors, personality traits, thought processes and into what inspires and motivates you. Knowing your wants and needs give you the power to align the action necessary to achieve what you want. When you practice self-awareness, control and improvement, your influence will increase and have a greater impact.

- Self-awareness allows a deeper understanding of your unique combination of strengths and weaknesses. Be diligent in assessing who you are to gain a better perspective of why you think, feel and behave the way you do. Learning what really makes you tick and being okay with what you uncover. A chance to reconcile issues and replace it with whatever your heart desires. Know, be, and love thyself.

- Self-control is a part of your growth. Recognize people, places and things that trigger emotions in you, and begin to gain control over your thoughts, feelings and behavior. Take back your power and never allow negative thoughts and emotions to overrule your better judgment. Operating in an emotionally mature state helps you become a better person, greater leader and communicator.

- Self-improvement is a never-ending process. Ideas, technology, relationships; they are constantly evolving. Explore outside of what is familiar for new ways to improve every area of your mind, body and spirit.

## THE PROCESS OF SELF-ASSESSMENT

Upgrade your lifestyle, knowledge, skillset and use them to create more opportunities to grow. Accept that there is always something you can do to make yourself and your life better. Always.

SELF-APPROVED

## CHAPTER 4:

# Allow Your Gifts Their Space

*"What you are is God's gift to you, what you become is your gift to God."*

—Hons Urs von Balthasar

What a powerful quote by Father Balthasar. Take a moment to really think about this quote on deeper level. Its meaning becomes clear; all that you are and everything you possess is given to you by God. Your talent, skills, and natural abilities are all gifts from God. You are a uniquely designed being, with purpose and intention weaved into your DNA. No one is identical to you in every way. Nope, not even if you are a twin. You may look identical, yet you have some physical and personality features that are just a tad different. Through self-discovery, you uncover your gifts and position them to work for you. The result is becoming the woman God created you to be.

I'm a December baby and love all things Christmas. Growing up in Texas, there were no white Christmases, no snow and very few cold days. I loved the transition from Thanksgiving to Christmas, when we decorated the tree with glass balls and strings of garland. I sat in the living room for hours, staring at the silver tree and multi-colored lights shining on it from the rotating color wheel. Its beauty promised me the most wonderful time of the year, and with it, a two-week vacation from school. I had long stopped believing in Santa, but I had expectation; somebody was getting me presents. Would I get what I wanted? Had I been good enough that year and did I do everything I was supposed to do?

One Christmas morning, my siblings and I ran downstairs and found all kinds of goodies and toys around the tree. As Mama began handing out presents, I spotted it: a large doll house with tiny dolls and matching furniture. My heart jumped out of my chest because I knew it was mine. I dreamt about that dollhouse and prayed to have it. It wasn't wrapped with a bow or hidden out of sight, and all I had to do was start playing. My other gifts, however, were tightly wrapped with layers of paper, tape and tissue. I opened the packaging just enough to peek inside, then went back to playing with the dollhouse. As the New Year rolled in, so did winter's cold and time to go back to school. I wondered, "What happened to the clothes I got for Christmas?" I pulled them from the closet and tore through the remaining layers of wrapping paper to get them out. Much to my surprise, what I thought was just clothes was a much warmer coat and sweaters. The house shoes, pajamas and a robe were the perfect fit for those chilly nights. The gifts I ignored were just what I needed to stay warm on the long walks to and from school.

Most often, your greatest gifts lie in what you are already passionate about. Other times, you stumble into them. Then there are those times when you must cut through layers of wrapping paper to get to them. The wrapping paper is everything holding you back, keeping you stuck and complacent in a life not designed for you. Have you heard the old saying, "What's yours is yours?" Well, it's true to a point. What's yours will become yours *if* you choose to accept it. When your gifts aren't obvious and you have to cut through layers of fear and social conditioning to uncover them, self-awareness is critical. Give yourself permission to fully explore beyond the familiar, to get out there and not just dabble. You know what it's like when you stick your big toe in to test the water before jumping in. If the water is cold, you might stop there instead of immersing yourself. Similarly, exploring your gifts presents a choice; a comfortable, warm and predictable lifestyle or a venture of curiosity into the unknown? It's a choice many people have difficulty making due to the demand of day-to-day survival. You may have good intentions, yet the daily *have-to's* increase offering little time to explore those good intentions. You put life in a holding pattern, at least until something happens that forces you to actively seek a better way.

Growing up, I wanted to be several things, including a teacher, chemist or a professional executive doing board member type stuff. When life happened and the *have-to's* took over, my focus shifted to getting a stable 9-5 job with good pay and benefits. Every effort went into maintaining a lifestyle for which there was no room for anything that might, possibly, maybe, even remotely jeopardize my income. So, I settled into a comfortable little box that began to close in around me. An overwhelming dissatisfaction with *normal* crept in and brought a yearning to do something more meaningful with my life and career. My gut said there was more. I could feel more but couldn't see more. I thought getting a teaching job on the side might put an end to the nagging feeling, so I excitedly applied for a teaching certification. Once I had it, nothing changed. It wasn't until a vacation with my now husband did I come to terms with this anxiety.

We traveled with a group of friends to Cabo San Lucas, Mexico, and stayed at a lovely resort on the beach for a week. The agenda was fun in the sun excursions, relaxation on the beach with the Kindle and taking in the local culture. From the very first day, my attraction to the water was overwhelming. There was something about the sound of the waves crashing against the shore that drew me in and soothed my anxious spirit. I spent a lot of time sitting out in the sand just listening. It finally happened—a place of quiet and calm reflection where I could convene with God, uninterrupted. My entire life came into focus. The accomplishments, failures, and things I thought about doing years back and what I ended up doing instead. And you know what, it wasn't a sad or painful experience at all. Instead, it was more of a reconciliation and tuning my heart in to what was still possible *if* I let go of everything I wanted to control. The choice to move out of complacency became clear and brought with it a peace I hadn't experienced in a long time. I mentioned to God that I didn't know what He was up to, but I was certainly up for the change.

Do you have a strange feeling in your gut that's nagging you? Something stirring that you can't quite put your finger on? It's part fear, anticipation and excitement—but mostly fear. It's your spirit saying there is more on the horizon if you dare to see past where you are. The universe is beckoning for your untapped potential. Don't ignore the urge. There is something amazing inside, a talent that you've ignored far too long.

The question becomes: how do you go about 1) recognizing, 2) developing and 3) operating in your gifts? I want to refresh your memory on what you've learned and implemented up to this point. With **Chapter one** you improved your self-esteem by changing how you saw yourself. You had a change in perspective. Past experiences became learning opportunities for what you want to do differently. You felt good about yourself, recognizing that you are valuable and deserve happiness. You easily visualized what you want and are now ready to go after it. Your outlook for the future became stronger than it's ever been and you are making a difference right where you are. In **Chapter two**, you saw how important it is to validate yourself from within and grow in confidence. You found inside of yourself the acceptance and appreciation you previously sought from others. You showed yourself grace, love and care as you moved forward. Now you are secure and comfortably embrace all that makes you uniquely different. **Chapter three** began your process of awareness, control and improvement. You walked through the *ICMe3*™ Principles of Self-Assessment with a deeper understanding of who you are, learning about your contributions, needs, triggers and how you show up every day. You know what it takes to be responsible and accountable to your dreams, standing up for you, to you.

Now the question is, "What's next?" Revisit and build upon the list you created in chapter three that represents your passion and what brings you joy. What would you do even if you didn't get paid for it? What about the things you do that are easy for you, even if you don't enjoy them? There may be opportunities to tweak what's not working to make it effective.

As you review new ideas, see how you've grown to overcome your circumstances. Think about times when you felt empowered and confident. What were you doing in those moments and what made them feel so special? Expand your imagination and envision ways to create more of those moments. Cultivate the power inside of you and allow it to open doors you may have been resistant to approach before. Here are a few things to consider as you begin to explore and develop your talent:

**What comes naturally for you?** Do you know someone who has never taken a singing lesson, yet their melodious voice flows out of them like water? Or someone who plays the piano so well that the first stroke of the keys sends goose bumps up your arm? They have no formal training, classes or anything—they just can? Or what about the person with an uncanny ability to make a stranger feel at right at home? It's a gift, the natural talent that requires little to no effort. Think about what came easy for you the first time you tried it. Even if you started a tad shaky, stay with it and give yourself time to sharpen the skill. Sometimes people give up on a talent because it didn't start off perfect and perky, so they feel discouraged. But remember, the more you use your talent, the stronger it becomes. It's like going to the gym and getting a workout. You build strength and endurance while pushing the limits to test all your gift can do. You are perfecting its capabilities, and in the process, you also build your confidence muscles.

**Listen to confirming voices.** Do the words of others bring confirmation to what you already feel in your gut? Have people whose opinion you value shared what a natural you are at "this or that," yet you dismissed the confirmation as nothing special? Explore these encouragers. They may be a huge advantage and resource to support your dream. Let me share an example. There was a guy in the neighborhood who cut his own hair to save money. He couldn't afford to be a regular at the barber shop, although he'd go a time or two. Others complimented how well a job he'd done cutting his own hair and asked if he would cut theirs. He did, and continued to practice cutting the hair of kids in the neighborhood whose parents couldn't afford the barbershop. The talent he used as a hobby supported his education, helped him get a barber's license and start his own business. God has a way of speaking to you through situations and the voice of others. If someone has complimented you on a talent you felt was irrelevant, take time to explore it thoroughly. Meditate and pray for revelation. Ask God for guidance and clarity, then yield to the confirmation you receive. Give it a try. You just might open the door to greater impact, potential revenue and a more fulfilling opportunity.

**Develop a heart of service.** The gifts you possess are not for your benefit alone; they are meant to build, strengthen, and uplift the lives of others. There are local organizations that will benefit from your skillset, so look for ways to volunteer in your community. Participate in fundraisers like 5k walks or food drives for causes in which you deeply believe. You could even organize an event to support organizations financially. Put your hands to work at shelters, pantries, or nursing homes. Community needs are great, so do your research for non-profit organizations whose work aligns with your core values. Don't worry if you have no volunteer experience, because most organizations will teach you what to do. Giving of yourself meets the need in all of us to be wanted, to feel as though we are helping someone else's life be better. In return, the lives of those you serve are greatly improved. Seek out ways to serve with what you've been given. Go out, meet new people and help someone who isn't as fortunate. One of my favorite quotes by Mahatma Ghandi said it best, *"The best way to find yourself is to lose yourself in the service of others."* Within your act of service lies the potential to uncover hidden talents in other areas of your life, which brings a fulfilling sense of peace and purpose.

**Disrespect fear.** Let's face it: fear will continue to exist and throw a monkey wrench in every goal you set. As you are exposed to new experiences, choose to believe what 2 Timothy 1:7 says, *"For God hath not given us the spirit of fear; but of power, and of love, and of a sound mind."* Fear will make you believe your plans won't work, that you are wasting your time because what you want is too far out of reach. When fear overtakes your thinking, it steals time and puts in its place a perpetual state of "waiting for it to be the right time." You can spend years buffering, spinning in circles and going nowhere. Don't wait list your purpose. Treat fear like a thief who's robbing you with a fake gun—it has no power except what you give it. Don't hand over your valuable gifts, talents or dreams to fear. You must not procrastinate if your confidence is shaken or when you experience a moment of doubt. Stir up the gifts inside you and exercise your faith. Use action to counter what fear whispers into your ear. The mere act of ***doing*** despite what fear says, concretes your commitment to be accountable to your dreams. Every time fear rears its ugly head, slap it in the face with the force of unbridled creativity. Let nothing impede your progress. Focus your time and energy on moving forward.

**Watch out for distractions.** People spend so much time doing things that don't serve any purpose. Those things are time and energy guzzlers that distract from what is important. They eventually become roadblocks that impede your progress. How do you identify distractions? Start with the basic things you do every day. I'm not talking about getting much deserved rest; I'm talking about those subtle distractions that you say will only take a few minutes. Here's an example: I work from home, so instead of working in my back office, I'm at the dining room table. I look up from the keyboard and notice dust on the ceiling fan. On my way to get the ladder from the garage, I pass through the laundry room. Well, of course I'll have to start a load of laundry, but before I can do that, I have to sort the clothes. An hour later, I still haven't cleaned that ceiling fan! The 5-10 minutes it should take for menial tasks will add up to hours wasted. They take you off track, cause a loss of focus and wreak havoc on your schedule. Social media is also a huge distraction: checking posts, tweets, pictures, likes, uploads, downloads, shares, comments or playing games. Constantly checking emails, notifications, text messages and phone calls are distractions as well. When you really need to focus, silence the notifications on your computer and phone. That way, you can focus and be intentional with your time. As you practice mitigating distractions, your effectiveness will increase. Very few things are as exciting as sitting down and getting something important accomplished.

Here's another form of distraction: people. Some people will see subtle changes in you or catch a glimpse that something is different about you. They may not see your potential or understand what you are doing. They won't get why you are no longer hanging out, talking badly about others, or doing things you once said were impossible. They may even be offended by the newly inspired and motivated you. Consequently, those once-comfortable friends don't fit in where you are going. While some will genuinely cheer for you, others may not, so be okay with the changes in you. If negative opinions come, don't take them personally. Never allow anyone to make you feel bad about yourself or question your desire for a better life. Deciding to change is better than stagnating. Stay the course and don't abort your progress or plan. Feed yourself a balanced diet of faith, courage and knowledge. Yes, you can really nurture your purpose by trusting yourself and connecting with people who encourage you. Make your gifts known and allow them to flourish. You hold the promises of God within to fulfill His design. Jeremiah 29:11 says, *"I know the plans I have for you, says The Lord. Plans to prosper you and not to harm you. Plans to give you hope and a future."* You owe it to yourself, and those you love, to become who God created you to be.

## Recap and Challenge

Destiny is not a destination; it's a journey. It doesn't matter what you went through. Your past doesn't define you or dictate what the future will hold. If you think it's too late to live your dream, or if feel there is nothing special about you, remember God endowed you with inalienable talent to use along your journey. It doesn't matter what age you are or which stage you are in life. You already have the victory. Do *you* in excellence and maintain your energy.

- Stay positive. You are creating impact right now in the space you're in, even if you don't see it. Keep moving,

## ALLOW YOUR GIFTS THEIR SPACE

knowing that your gifts will sustain and make room for you.

- Listen to the voices that most align with what you believe about yourself. You will know when words spoken aren't for your gain. Self-awareness and instinct does this for you.

- Be open to serving others in some capacity. Opening your heart to give in this way stirs new desire and passion you might not have exposure to otherwise.

- Grow—in spite of fear—stretch yourself to believe past what you see. Limit your access to anything that distract from your mission. Surround yourself with people who are growing in their space as much as you are in yours. #Support

As abundance overflows in your life and overtakes you, I challenge you to connect *one* of your gifts to a need in your community. Go out and see how you can be a blessing with what you have. Continue to allow your gifts to show up authentically every day, and stay the course until you have birthed everything God put in you.

SELF-APPROVED

CHAPTER 5:

# Subscribe to Self-Care Therapy

*"I have come to believe that caring for myself is not self-indulgent. Caring for myself is an act of survival."*

—Audre Lorde

You wake up feeling refreshed and excited today. What a great night's sleep you had as you bounce out of bed, stretch, and breathe in the fresh scent of lavender flowers. Throwing back the curtains, you feel the warmth of sunshine as it fills the room. The birds are chirping and the automatic coffee maker is brewing your favorite breakfast blend. It's time to jump in the shower, get dressed and meet the kids at the front door, eager to start the day. Oh my goodness, what a wonderful day you'll have, with no conflict at work, everyone getting along, all deadlines met and on the Fast Track for a promotion. You breeze through every green light on the way home, where you will find the kids have done their homework and dinner is served. You relax in the tub with a good book, and as you snuggle under the covers that night, your mind is so clear that you waste no time falling into a deep, peaceful sleep.

Really? No, not really; it's probably more like this: You wake up in a panic because you overslept. For some reason, you don't hear the alarm go off. You shower with lightning speed, drag the kids out of bed and run out of the house with no coffee, smack dab into rush hour traffic. It's gridlocked and now you're late. Finally at your desk, the anxiety builds as you scour and prioritize the e-mails in order of importance. The coworker in the next cubicle has issues and your much-needed raise is delayed due to budget cuts. Lunch break consists of a few bites of a microwaved something at the desk and you're counting the minutes until quitting time. After work you're back in rush hour traffic, heading home with drive-thru dinner in hand. You pick up the house, help with homework, and spend time with the family. As you snuggle into bed exhausted, your mind kicks into high gear with a list of chores you ***didn't*** get around to doing.

More realistic? Definitely. So, you will relate to this saying, "Man may work from sun to sun but a woman's work is never done." I don't know who came up with this quote, but it continues to ring true in the lives of women every day. It doesn't matter if you work outside of the home or not; the demands of time and energy will wreak havoc on your health if you are not careful. There are women who work outside the home, yet still manage the kids, household and spouses in addition to caring for aging parents. There are single mothers standing in the gap for absent fathers and women who assumed responsibility for children they didn't bear, all with little to no support system.

As a single mom, missing work was not an option for me. I was at work—rain, sleet or snow. If I needed time off for doctor appointments or to pop-in on the kids at school, I stayed late the next day to make up the time. Vacation days were rarely used for vacations and reserved for when I or the kids were sick. This "Wonder Woman®" mentality kept me in overdrive and running on fumes most days, with no regard for self-care.

Effective self-care is not much different from what you do for others and requires little time or money. It's just a matter of shifting a bit of your focus to see yourself as important as you see everything else on your to-do list. Face it, many of the things you want to do will get half-done if you are not fully present or feeling your best. That's because it's difficult to stay positive and polite when you lack rest. It's true. How many times have you snapped angrily at someone because you were tired? Patience went out the window and you mumble those infamous words, "They are getting on my last nerve!" Physical, mental and emotional rest is necessary for maintaining the fortitude to push through obstacles. Exhaustion affects your ability to remain confident and increases the chances of depression. That is serious business. Instead of continuing to run on fumes, change the way you do things by learning and listening to what your body needs. It has a way of speaking to you during moments of stress and fatigue with signs that include headache, tension, low energy, chest pain or recurring colds and infections.

If left unchecked, these symptoms can lead to illnesses of a greater concern. Make self-care a priority now instead of waiting until you're flat on your back thinking, *I have to take better care of myself.* I've mumbled those words many times over the years, when I exhausted my immune system, it broke down and caught the flu. There was always something to do—work, church, school, home, kids' school activities and events—you name it. Plus, I had my hands in everyone else's business and was running around with my Wonder Woman cape on, ready to save the day. The flu came out of nowhere. One day I was running errands, and the next day I was so weak it was a struggle to get out of bed. As much as I love food, the smell of it made me sick. I'd muster enough strength to get the kids to school, then right back in the bed I went. After a week out of commission, I forced myself to get up and go back to work.

Once there, I spent the entire week with my head on the desk and my supervisor didn't complain. After recovering, I realized the flu didn't come out of nowhere. The headaches, sluggishness and inability to focus were signs my body needed rest—signs that I wasn't taking good care of myself, signs I ignored. I accepted that it wasn't necessary to run myself into the ground to prove I was a good mother, employee, church member, student, friend or anything else. It was unrealistic to be all things to everyone in every situation. I needed to take care of me, my own business, and let others take care of theirs. So before things get out of hand for you, give yourself care therapy. Look at areas of your life where you are putting your needs on the back burner. See the places where you are stretched entirely too thin and your energy is fading. Be honest—you know what they are. Think about the things you dread doing but know you must do. How can you make these tasks less taxing? Decide today to treat yourself better, to allow your body time to rebuild and increase the time you spend doing what brings you pleasure and peace.

> *"Taking good care of you means the people in your life will receive the best of you, rather than what's left of you."*
>
> —Carl Bryan

Self-care and love are the necessary building blocks for confidence, strength and courage. This is true, not only for everyday preservation, but for increasing the chances that you're able to endure for the long term. That means staying healthy by going to the doctor for regular checkups, mammograms and pap smears, and to the dentist for healthy teeth and gums. It means loving yourself enough to realize when you're over-worked. It makes no sense to be so exhausted that you can't think straight, yet you still push. Take a moment to rest your mind so you can fully engage and get stuff done. It means minimizing stress where you can. No matter how hard you try to focus, if you are stressed in one area of your life, stress will ultimately affect other areas. How often have you underperformed at work because of personal issues at home? Or took work home at the end of the day because you were spread too thin? You can bring greater synergy to your life by creating a plan of action that starts with your overall well-being. Make self-care non-negotiable and consider the following guidelines "must-do's" that support giving yourself a break and doing what's good for your body, mind and spirit:

**Set and maintain personal boundaries.**

Boundaries are not meant to separate you from others, keep people out or you boxed in…although sometimes removing yourself from negative energy is a darn good thing. Having boundaries in place maintains the health and quality of your space. Lack of boundaries becomes a problem when you're taught to sacrifice what you want for the sake of making others happy. With everything pulling at your time, it's easy for others to become dependent on you for things they can realistically do for themselves. Consequently, creating and reinforcing your personal boundaries helps others rise to a higher level of awareness and management for their own lives and allows your influence to support their growth. It's okay to say *no*, or at least *not now* to the wants of others—especially when saying *yes* creates undue sacrifice on you or your time.

Do you find yourself in any one of these situations?

- Do you feel as if people take advantage of you or use your emotions for their own gain, through guilt, manipulation or bullying?
- Have you ever felt as if you are constantly rescuing others or fixing their problems?
- Are you frustrated with defending yourself, your values or your decisions against people who dictate what you should be doing and how?

These are examples of either having no boundaries or having boundaries you may not be enforcing. Your energy and emotions are used up as you try to be nice, accepted and liked. You can't always shoulder the responsibility of others, and in trying to rescue them, you become their safety net. What you *can* do is support them in managing their own issues.

I struggled in this area for a while. I had frequent requests for time and money, and most often I gave without much of either to spare. The loan became a gift when they didn't repay me, and it left me scrambling to pay the bills. After pulling my hair out trying to make ends meet, I decided to stop being other people's bailout. I had to stick to my own rules: 1) give if I have it and it doesn't put my expenses in jeopardy, 2) if they didn't pay back the first time, loan no more and 3) never co-sign another anything that doesn't directly affect me. The first time I said *no* to extending another loan, it was nerve wrecking. I felt bad to be in a position where saying no was necessary, and I knew from experience this person wouldn't be happy about it. As I laid out all the reasons why my answer was no, I became angry that they felt explaining was necessary. I mean, seriously—they hadn't paid back the money I loaned them the first time but they still had the audacity to be upset? I stuck to my guns and we both hung up the phone angry. Although saying no was the right thing to do, after calming down a bit, I felt uncomfortably guilty and wondered how they would make it without my help. I pushed through it and forced myself not to inquire. It took a few months before that person spoke to me again, but I was pleased to find out their world didn't end and they met their own financial needs. Enforcing your boundaries with money allows others to become self-sufficient, make better personal choices and removes a huge weight off your shoulders. Saying no takes practice. You may feel guilty at first, but push through it. You will relieve so much stress when you reinforce boundaries, and others will begin to respect your boundaries as well.

## Write "me" time in your schedule.

If you are one of those ladies who does everything by your planner, add yourself to the calendar instead of waiting for time to open up. Write it in ink so it's non-negotiable and not easily erased. If it seems odd to take time for yourself, start with five to ten minutes a day to get in the habit. You can build upon those minutes as you start enjoying those precious moments—trust me, you will. The key to self-care is consistency. Whether it's reading a few chapters of a good book, taking lunch away from the desk or a brisk walk around the neighborhood, keep the appointment with yourself, no matter what. No one gets your time, and no other task can take its place.

My first intentional *me* time came with an overwhelming feeling that I should be doing something. It was early one Saturday morning as I sat on the back porch with a cup of coffee. I sat there instead of starting the weekend with my usual housecleaning ritual. Instead, I forced myself to relax and enjoy quiet time, doing nothing. I loved the smell of the clean early morning dew, but this felt so—wrong. I was doing nothing when there was so much to do. I continued to sit there and watch the birds, sip my coffee and was soon lost in thought. I only planned to be out there a few minutes, but it turned into several coffee refills and a day of laying around the house watching old movies. And **that** felt good. The next day I had more energy for the first time in a long time and completed everything I wanted to do over that weekend.

Despite what you've heard, self-care is not selfish, nor is it arrogant to believe you deserve to intentionally take time for yourself. Re-think what self-care looks and feels like for you. Be proactive and create a list of tactics you can whip out of your arsenal when you're limited on time and money. Self-care does not always involve money. A walk in the park, work in the yard or anything that will help you feel special and rejuvenated. Set a price point and a "how often" so you are prepared. Going to the spa or having manicures and pedicures are great rejuvenators, but if you can't afford it, pamper yourself at home. Do-it-yourself treatments can give salon-like quality for a fraction of the price. Girl time out with special friends is therapeutic as well, if you find pleasure and fulfillment from it.

Spend time getting your thoughts out of your head and emotions out of your heart, and onto paper by journaling. If you had a diary as a child, it's doing the exact same thing. Purchase a journal, diary or notebook and write out thoughts and feelings about any and everything you want. If you prefer journaling on a smartphone or tablet, I recommend downloading an app you can use to capture and manage your words. This is your private space to share the intimate details of your life that you might not share with anyone. It could be anything! Think about what's happening in your day, moments that made you excited, or even those that left you anxious and frustrated. Journaling helps to release those moments onto paper, instead of upside someone's head. Release the pent-up pain of the past that you've prayed about and haven't been able to fully let go. Pour it out on paper. It's a therapeutic and cleansing way to rid yourself of negative energy, opening the door for healing and restoration. It's not just for you—sharing your life experiences can heal others if you decide to publish the works, poems and thoughts of your journal. Consider sharing your story.

**Develop healthy habits.**

Putting yourself first does not mean you're putting anyone else last. It's a commitment to taking care of yourself properly so you have the energy to do the things you love. Establish criteria for what's good for your body, mental and emotional well-being, and activate these self-care practices:

- **Prayer** helps you stay connected and grounded in God. Make time for daily communion in His presence. Give thanks for everything your heart is grateful for and embrace His guidance, direction and purpose for your life.

- **Meditation** keeps you centered and focused with self. Bring calm and peace into your space and release any negativity. See your life clearly.

- **Journaling** cleanses your mind and spirit by having a place to dump your thoughts and ideas. This is a healing place where you can release stress and frustration. Your words are kept between you, God and the paper—unless you decide to publish your collection.

- **Proper** diet gives your body the vitamins and minerals it needs to function properly. Eat your vegetables (in my mama voice) and drink lots of water.

- **Physical** activity rids your body of toxic stress and gives you energy. Engage in exercise to strengthen your heart and muscles and keep your body strong.

- **Stretching** reduces stress on the body, improves posture, relieves pain and releases endorphins in the brain to improve your mood and ward off depression. It also helps to keep your limbs flexible.

- **Spend** time with people you can relax and be yourself with, those who love and support you with no pretense or expectations.

- **Lighten up**—laughter is the best medicine and one of the best ways to reduce stress and boost your immune system.

- **Travel** to other places and see the "big beautiful" God gave you. A change of scenery is always rejuvenating for your senses and gaining new perspective.

## SUBSCRIBE TO SELF-CARE THERAPY

- **Learn** something new and interesting. Learning keeps your mind sharp. You may just uncover a hidden talent while exploring ways to grow yourself.

- **Pamper** yourself. What better way to show yourself love than by getting a massage, facial, a mani/pedi or a new hairdo? At home or at the spa, it doesn't matter. The refreshing rejuvenation does.

- **Play** more. It's an opportunity to be a kid for a bit. Do silly stuff—amusement parks, dancing in the rain, catching fireflies—not even the sky's the limit on the laughs you'll have. Just don't ring the neighbor's door bell and run. ☺

- **Take** up a hobby. Throw yourself into an activity just for fun. Play the piano, paint, crafting, sewing—what have you always wanted to try?

- **Volunteer**. The giving of yourself in the act of service to others provides an overwhelming sense of purpose and connectedness to your fellow man (or woman).

- **Do** more of what you enjoy. Above everything else, do *more* of what brings you joy, happiness and peace. And do it often.

Woman, you have an innate ability to care for any and every one you encounter, which leaves self-care on the back burner more times than not. You go above and beyond the call of duty to ensure the T's are crossed and I's are dotted daily. You are a blessing beyond measure, and your selfless service is important to the lives you touch.

## Recap and Challenge

There are a few things to realize: you cannot give to others effectively what you don't give yourself. *"Love your neighbor the same __as__ you love yourself,"*—Matthew 19:19 ERV. The word 'as' is a critical conjunction in this statement, because it shows that Jesus meant loving your neighbor "in addition to" loving yourself. Don't take you out of the equation because you're caring for others, and resist feeling guilty taking time to focus on you.

I challenge you to create a lifestyle of healthy habits. Be honest about where you stand in your personal care. Have a look at everything you pour yourself out for, and commit to pouring back into you. If you've slacked off in the past, start today by making yourself a priority. Giving your body, mind and spirit rest and relaxation improves your health, can ward off diseases, and helps with your tenacity to withstand the challenges life throws at you. You were meant to enjoy life and live in abundance as you live out and in your purpose.

SUBSCRIBE TO SELF-CARE THERAPY

SELF-APPROVED

## CHAPTER 6:

# Turn Your Vision into Action

*"Create the highest, grandest vision possible for your life, because you become what you believe."*

—Oprah Winfrey

You can accomplish anything you want in life by putting fear aside and just going for it. Maybe fear isn't the right word for your situation—how about procrastination, laziness, apprehension, anxiety or over-analyzing? Could it be you're afraid to fail or the possibility of having what you want is a bit intimidating? Maybe it's lack of resources you are unsure about, or you're reluctant to dream again or to start over, after what you tried before failed. You gave everything, and maybe you don't believe you have the strength...or the will… to keep going. It's understandable when you've been hurt and abused, that you get tired of fighting for change. But if your triumph is in your next move, you won't find it if you quit. Muster up enough strength to try again. Dare to believe and trust the gifts God put in you. Allow Him to resurrect everything you thought was dead. Let faith and vision motivate you to push through complacency and stagnation. God didn't bring you this far for you to quit on what you are meant to accomplish. Trust in yourself and give yourself another chance. You can win your way if you just keep believing.

Most people desperately want to do more in their lives, yet they can't find the strength or motivation to push through whatever circumstances they face, so they stop short of the goal line. I remember I had so many excuses they fit every degree on the thermometer. When life got really hot, I was creative and molded excuses to fit my lack of commitment. The fact is, there is **no** excuse under the sun that is good enough to stop any of us from doing better, or having a desire for a better life and going after it. I want you to stop for a moment and imagine what life looks like beyond the situation that's holding you back. See beyond fear and lack of resources.

Seriously—lay down the book for a moment, find a quiet place, take a deep breath, close your eyes and think about **one** thing you've been dreaming about. Just one thing. Don't overwhelm this process. Don't think about what went wrong before. Forget about your current problems or limits. Use the power of your imagination to think about what you want, as if it *is* happening.

Relax and see it clearly. Engage your senses and go in further. Visualize what it looks like with you standing smack dab in the middle of it. Embrace the beauty—it's everything you hoped it would be, and you're making your impact exactly as you intended. Your life is changing as a result, right before your eyes. Watch as doors of opportunity and blessing swing open in your favor. There is no sky. There is no limit. It doesn't matter where you started. It doesn't matter where you came from. Your past does not dictate your future. You are not too late, or too old, or too (fill in the blank). You have everything you need and always have. You are this vision—this vision is you and it's in you. Dreaming in color brings your vision to life with meaning and increases hope and possibility. Fear gives way to faith and confidence. Brainstorming replaces procrastination. Living as if your dreams are denied is no longer an option. You've had a glimpse of what's possible, so there's no more stumbling into your purpose by happenstance. It's not enough to be excited about putting a vision together. You must execute on it by creating a plan of actionable items to bring your vision to fruition.

## Clarity is key.

If it was challenging to walk through the exercise at the beginning of this chapter, you may need more time to get clear on the outcome you desire. Especially if you have been overly obsessed with the *how to get it done* part, your mind will want to focus on the details without a clear picture of the outcome. For instance, if your dream is to speak professionally, focus on the outcome you want. See yourself standing in front of an eager audience, and your speech is achieving the result you desire. You are in demand, and your calendar is booked with recurring events. Each speaking engagement brings even more opportunities to speak. At this point, it doesn't matter what your talk was about, who's in the audience or how large of a crowd you spoke to. Envisioning yourself doing what you want is what matters. The details will come during the planning stage.

Establishing your goals doesn't just answer the questions what and how, it also identifies your why. Asking yourself why you want this thing ensures you're not taking on someone else's vision or following their plan for your life. Consider what's important about this goal and what value it will it add to your life or the life of someone else. How does it align with the mission and purpose you're working towards and what will it cost you in time, money, resources and/or relationships? Yes, there will be investments and sacrifices involved, not just for you but for those who journey with you, such as your family and friends. It may be necessary to distance yourself from people who speak against your success. Keeping these items in mind mitigates distractions, delays and detours, as you progress through the execution stage of your goal. Make sure you are clear, concise and focused on moving your vision from dreaming about it to living it. Goals aren't just things to accomplish; they become how you *do* life and they hone the process for achieving future goals.

## What's your intention?

Not every goal has to be deep or detail oriented; some are as simple as scheduling time one day a week to clean, exercise or go to the market. They require very little mind work or preparation, but you'll still want to add them to your calendar to allow time to get them done along with everything else. What about in the workplace? Your goal can be to have a meeting with your team every morning. Basic and simple goals. For more detailed planning, I'm sure you've heard about setting S.M.A.R.T. goals, using a strategy of planning, measuring and achieving a goal; being *smart* about the process. According to Google, there are many suggested terms representing the S.M.A.R.T. acronym:

- Specific—having a target or something specific to achieve.
- Measurable—a way to measure what is being achieved along the way.

- Agreed-upon—everyone involved is in agreement with what's necessary.
- Realistic—with resources being used to decide if the goal can be achieved.
- Time bound—is there enough time or time limit set for completion of each step?

The definitions will vary depending on who you ask, but, in essence, the S.M.A.R.T. process takes into account the logistics of a goal and the coordination of people, time and resources. What it falls short in answering is whether the goal is aligned with the purpose and vision you've designed for your life. I can't count how many times I started working on something, only to realize midstream that it wasn't really what I wanted. I was easily influenced by others and too busy caught up in pretending I was someone I wasn't. In an effort to please people, I found myself performing tasks important to them. With no passion for it, the goal ended up looking more like a hobby.

Think about what you've been saddled with: Did you come from a generation of (insert any profession) and the *family* expectation is for you to follow the same path? Oh man, that's a huge amount of guilt and pressure, especially if what you want is significantly different from the family's plan. Are you struggling to prove you can live up to their expectations, even if they're not what you want? Following others' footsteps is an important pathway forward, with them having paved the way through most obstacles. As you grow and mature, it's time to place your own footprints in the sand and pave your own way. You won't just be creating goals, you'll be creating a life. You'll need to spend some time working through what's right for you when deciding what to undertake. I've created a variation of S.M.A.R.T. that focus on qualities to consider in advance. It's a way to vet the goal, vision, or project **before** you invest your time in laying out the specific, measurable, agreed-upon, relevant and time-bound details. In this paradigm, S.M.A.R.T. stands for Substance, Merit, Authentic, Relevant and Tangible.

**S = Substance**: What is the goal made of? What quality elements does it have or value will it add to your life's achievements? Forget the glitz and glamour; does it have purpose, meaning and can it easily sustain your attention when life throws you off track? *Example*: College isn't for everyone, so trying to pursue a degree holds no value when you don't like the structure of classroom learning. While furthering your education is an important goal, explore other learning experiences besides going to college. Good intentions won't be enough to sustain your passion; your goal must have substance that's relevant for you.

**M = Merit**: Is this goal credible and worthy of the time, energy and effort you will have to invest? What good will having it provide, and is there a level of integrity or moral principle driving it? *Example*: I met a beautiful young lady; she was smart, talented and as sweet as pie. She wanted to be married with kids, which is a great goal, right? Wrong! She wanted to be married to someone else's husband, and spent a lot of time thinking what her life would be like when they could finally be together. She didn't understand her worth, and did anything she could to make him leave his wife. Her goal lacked a moral compass and created enormous problems for her, investing her time, energy and heart into something she could not attain. (No, he didn't leave his wife.)

**A = Authentic**: How genuine is this goal for you? How does it feel in the overall scheme of your plan? Is it your sincere desire to bring this goal to life, and not someone else pushing their agenda on you? Have you ever said, "I don't know why I'm doing this; it ain't even me?" Many goals don't work because you're trying to do things that don't fit your style, personality or heart. Authenticity is the fertile soil that gives your goals life, richness and pureness of deed. Properly cultivated, goals allow your heart and passion to show through. You will know the truth by how it feels in what you do. Follow your gut instinct. What you want *will* work if you'll just be yourself, operate in your own talent and stay true to your purpose. Don't be distracted by the glitter of fads.

**R = Relevance**: How important is the goal to your bigger picture? Can it keep you passionately engaged and motivated while providing the basis to establish future goals? *Example*: I worked for a telecommunications company for more than 27 years, and at one point did customer service work. I was on a mission to learn as much as possible by transferring to different jobs within the company. I took a physical test to become an outside technician and failed the first time because I didn't have upper body strength. I worked out, did pushups and lifted weights so I'd be ready to retake and pass the next exam six months later. The training to strengthen my body was a six-month goal, relevant in order to pass the test and get the job I wanted. The effects of that goal got me the job, which was the basis (and provided the skill necessary) for every position I held afterwards.

**T = Tangible**: How touchable is the goal? While it can definitely be a stretch, a goal can't be so far-fetched that it frustrates you during the time it takes to achieve it. ***Example***: The thought of earning a million dollars is fantastic, but how realistic is it in relation to where you are in your current financial position? Unlike hitting the lottery, success isn't instant, nor should be played as a game of chance. Becoming a millionaire can be a goal divided into bite-sized financial milestones gained over a period of time. That way, you stay engaged with mini-goals to celebrate along the way.

How many goals do you want to accomplish over your lifetime, and what areas of your life do they affect? There are six main areas that revolve around you—personal, relationships, lifestyle, health and well-being, financial security and career goals. While you are laying out your goals, align your vision. As you are making plans, take a step back and see the bigger picture of how one area of your life affects another.

## TURN YOUR VISION INTO ACTION

Most of your goals will overlap or build upon each other. For instance, if you want to purchase a home, you may need to save money for a down payment or rebuild your credit. Both money and credit repair are smaller goals that must happen first in order to attain the larger goal of buying a house. This creates a cycle of planning that results in a lifestyle plan. Purchasing a home affects three areas of life: finances, personal, lifestyle and possibly your career choices. While you lay out the goals for different areas, remember their overall effect. Success in one area can create success in another; the same holds true for frustration and chaos. Make sure your goals are aligned with your overall well-being.

**Personal**
- Spiritually.
- Ideal emotional state.
- Legacy.

**Relationship** | With self and others
- Family.
- Work place.
- Community.

**Lifestyle**
- Relaxation.
- Hobbies.
- Philanthropy.

**Health**
- Diet and exercise.
- Mental wellbeing.
- Personal care.

**Finances**
- Income/debt level.
- Security/Retirement.
- Charitable contribution.

**Career**
- Promotion.
- Networking.
- Entrepreneurship.

In order to create a lifestyle plan, start with what you know about you. What is your history and how can you use it to catapult you into the life you want? Look where you are today and where you want to be in the future, working in one area at a time.

Considering both perspectives of *smart* goals we've discussed, including logistics and goal quality, begin mapping out your thoughts now. To get you started, take a moment and identify *ONE* goal you want to accomplish within the next six months. Write it here:

_____

_____

Why is this goal important?

_____

_____

_____

_____

Now that you've specified the goal and why it's important, the next step is to research the resources you need. That includes talking to others who have done what you want to do. People are a resource most leave untapped; remember, you can't achieve goals alone, so reach out and build relationships with others before you need the help. Factor in a reasonable budget for both time and money, and set a realistic timeline for completion. Take personal responsibility for staying on track with your goals. If you find something you implemented isn't working just right, make an adjustment and keep pushing forward. It's okay to have a Plan B, C or D. I've heard before that having back-ups to Plan A means you are admitting failure of Plan A. That's a bunch of crock. Even the best and carefully laid plans go awry. You must be flexible in your thinking, being and doing, to shift or make necessary adjustments. It does not mean you are not committed to Plan A; it means you don't waste valuable time forcing what is not working. It's okay to pause often during the execution process to see what's not working according to plan, fix it and continue.

**Recap and Challenge**

Clarity is the key to fortifying goals and creating your life map. Trust in the process of purpose, planning, your passion and persistence, and allow them to fill every crevice of your being with possibility. If you have not identified the *one* goal you want to accomplish in the next six months, I challenge you to do it now. Go all in to make it happen. Remember, your way is already made for you. Believe the purpose you were given and allow yourself the grace of flowing in your authentic space. You have the tenacity to achieve your goals, so have faith in knowing that greater success is ahead. Be passionate, consistent and persistent in staying the course. These qualities go hand in hand, and will keep you focused when distractions come, and they will. Even if you hit a roadblock, snag or speed bump, allow yourself grace to re-group and start again. That you keep showing up is what's important. Keep it moving.

SELF-APPROVED

## CHAPTER 7:

# Build Relationships That Work

*"Alone we can do so little. Together we can do so much."*

—Helen Keller

Let me share a question I want you to think about. I read it on the website of a non-profit organization called The Relationship Foundation and it says, *"We spend at least 12 years in school preparing for a Career. How much time do you actually spend preparing for relationships, any relationship?"* The question made me reflect on the relationships I had in the past, and how I hooked up with people in the first place. I haven't always been in a place of wanting a relationship, or friendships, or just people to hang out with. I told myself many times how much I didn't like people. It was painful to give everyone what they wanted, when everyone wanted something different. People always ***want*** something! Money, time, a listening ear  then after they dumped their world of depression on me, I held onto the heaviness, trying to figure out how to help while they skipped off into the sunset. It seemed more trouble than it was worth, and I began to close myself off to people. Conversations became taxing and I tuned out, pretending to be interested by throwing in an occasional nod or grunt. Truth be told, it wasn't necessarily the people, it was more the drama or dependent behavior they brought with them. At times, it was extremely challenging to gather enough strength to allow others into my space. Yet, as I watched others flourish in their relationships, I couldn't help but wonder what was wrong with mine.

In looking over past relationships, I had silenced my needs and focused on those of others. Trying to be all things to all people led to two failed marriages and the number of friends I could count on one hand. I often held my tongue instead of speaking up for myself, thinking good relationships equaled self-sacrifice. I became fearful, anxious and withdrawn, and didn't trust anybody to get too close. I was afraid of not living up to the expectations of others, so when opportunities to meet new people were presented, I stood in the background watching, but saying nothing. I would think to myself, "she seems like a nice lady, but……" or "that group over there is having fun—I should go over and make friends but…"

When I was at work, I didn't have to make friends. I was there to do a job. I did my job and learned great customer service skills in the process. You know how the customer is always right? I became a team player and gained applause for a job well done. When I met my quota, everyone was happy. For the most part, the relationships I built at work stayed at work, except for a handful of people I am still friends with today. What made my relationships with them different from the others? I believe it was because we moved past work conversations into genuine interest. We spoke about issues without the fear of being liked or disliked. Our initial interactions at work led to having lunch individually or as a group, and then developed into close friendships outside of work.

So, how do you prepare for relationships? Lord help if it takes 12 years to complete a course in Relationship Building 101. Ain't nobody got time for 12 years! So, in most of my relationships that took a long time to develop, I realized my behavior made the difference. When I wasn't pretending to be someone I wasn't, the relationships worked, such as those at work. And it wasn't as simple as following the golden rule by treating others the way I wanted to be treated. There were times when the treatment I received was devoid of the care and concern I gave. And you know what's interesting? I discovered you really can't treat others the way you want to be treated, because not everyone has the same needs as you. Not everyone wants warm and fuzzy; some want straight shooting and facts. Some don't care about a back-story, while others want every detail. Knowing what to give people can be a game of chance, especially if they don't know themselves.

Obviously, I was missing something, so I became a fly on the wall of other people's interactions. I wasn't eavesdropping; I was just increasing my observation skills and gathering information to improve my skills at building relationships. Listening to conversations in many situations over a variety of topics began to change my perspective about the drama I dreaded. I watched body language, thought about the choice of words they used and observed how each party expressed themselves. Most times, no one person dominated the conversation, and I loved the flow of good energy that allowed the give, take and sharing of ideas. Even during heated discussions that made me apprehensive, people didn't appear angry or overly irritated with each other. Those conversations didn't end in a shouting match, and they wrapped up always laughing, still friends and agreeing to disagree. As you'd have it, disagreements don't have to mean a death sentence for the relationship. I wanted to stop being fearful, and expand my space to grow a network of friends and collaborators. This would be crucial to help me grow personally and professionally. I built the courage to open myself to good, strong, solid relationships based on what I wanted them to look and feel like. I combined what I learned into a system that works and provides realistic results. Having experienced my own diverse conversations gave me a few basic elements about good relationships:

- Everyone will have an opinion different from yours. Listen first to understand.

- Healthy alliances are not one-sided. Treat each other as equals, regardless of position.

- Solid relationships are based on mutual respect and inclusivity.

- Relationships can be a safe haven for supportive brainstorming and honest feedback.

- People make relationships more complicated than necessary. They really aren't.

- Awareness is critical. Everyone involved can have their needs met.

- Good relationships can strengthen your confidence and influence.

With zero preparation or training in how to relate to others, most people haphazardly assume that simply being nice is the key to a good relationship. In fact, most of what you've been told about having good relationships is completely wrong. I'm sure you've heard them too: "Be nice and agreeable, don't question authority, be ready to compromise, always help others and stay in your place." These are extremely generic concepts that create a complacent culture. You must have boundaries that prevent those you help from becoming dependent on you for things they can do themselves. What happens when you're always agreeable, or resist challenging authority? Should you compromise on something you hold dear, such as a core value or a deep belief, or take an oath to perform work you disagree with? Certainly not. What I do know is good relationships don't just happen. They are *heart* work and challenging at times, but well worth the effort. Trusting people after you've been hurt takes strength and courage. Have no fear. You are worthy of having healthy relationships, complete with mutual love and respect. No matter how many relationships you've had that didn't work out—marriages, friendships, family fallouts, business deals gone bad—you can still align yourself with good relationships and be comfortable in your life's journey. As your relationships grow, you will discover new talents, and pull out some you hid away years ago, and use them in ways you never imagined.

## Five personal strategies to build good relationships

My personal mission is to support you in bringing synergy to your life and business relationships. I know the power of partnerships and collaborations. Forging good relationships can heal the brokenness that is created by failed ones. I want to see every life blossom with the blessings of being connected to God, self and others. My life experiences, through mistakes, trial and error and relationship success, have taught me many things. If I can experience success in this area, so can you.

1. **Start with you.** Self-assessment includes awareness, management and improvement of *You* as the vital part of any relationship. Rely on the self-awareness process that you walked through at the beginning of this book. Your understanding and acceptance of who you are will dictate what you are willing to give and accept in any relationship. Show up with a level of maturity that gives value, authenticity, and growth to your partnerships. Be confident in what you bring to the table and secure in asking for what you need (and expect to receive) in your interactions with others. Remember, there is no sense in comparing yourself to others. Accept the brilliance of others who shine where you don't. Be in complement, not competition or jockeying for position. Your gifts, talent and presence will make room for you, so it's not necessary to connect yourself to people who do not value your contributions. Even in situations that trigger negative feelings can be managed with grace and ease when you are emotionally secure. This is an opportunity to see how much you have grown in being able to self-manage. When situations escalate, you don't have to.

2. **Respect individuality** in yourself and others. Stand out by standing up for who you are and what you believe. Resist the urge to blend in when it's comfortable. No one has what you have, in the same way you have it.

No other human being can do what you do, the way you do it. Allow your combination of strengths, weaknesses, qualities, thoughts, behaviors, ideas, creativity, experiences and talents to create a place where you automatically fit. Be comfortable in your skin, and let your quirkiness show through. You are a breath of fresh air, an original in a world of carbon copies. Respectively, honor the uniqueness of others for the strength, skill, talent and value they bring, and allow them to flourish as well. You are an individual with a personality, your partner or partners are individuals with personality, and when you come together, the relationship itself has a personality. Respecting individuality allows every aspect to thrive.

3. **Communication is essential**—communicate in a way that confidently shares your needs. As your confidence grows in the awareness of your needs, you're in a better position to communicate your needs effectively to others. How do you do this? It's a matter of opening your mouth. Sounds easy, right? It's not if you've been conditioned to put the needs of others before your own. Asking for something may feel strange at first, so this level of communication takes practice. It takes confidence and self-assurance to know that you deserve what you want, and have the expectation of receiving it. If you think people will automatically know how you feel, realize that folk aren't mind readers, and their awareness may not be as prevalent as yours to pick up on things. The only way for them to know is for you to express it. Be clear and confident in your "ask." Rephrase or

paraphrase. Get feedback to make sure there is no misunderstanding between you. If you're unsure how to share without over-sharing, especially in a space where vulnerability may be taboo, ask yourself: at what point am I uncomfortable providing more detail? What do I want to gain by sharing? Is it beneficial in any way to the situation? When others share openly and you think it's a bit too much, it's because over-sharing can be a way to validate an insecurity of some sort. For instance, when I struggled in a previous marriage, I often discussed it with a colleague. The more I shared, the less she sympathized. Me, glad to have someone to talk with, shared more intimate details than were necessary. I wanted an outlet. I wanted someone to say I was right. Having a sympathetic ear made the dysfunction feel better. This was definitely conversation for a best friend, not a colleague. I learned it's totally okay to keep some private things between you and God. Any time you're uncomfortable sharing, don't do it. Remember your personal boundaries and develop the ability to say *no* clearly if someone else's ask doesn't align with your purpose. It's okay to say "not now" instead for those times when saying yes may stretch your resources.

4. **Strive for quality** over quantity as the basis for establishing relationships. I know the pull to be liked and followed is attractive and addicting, especially if you're an entrepreneur, where building a large audience of potential customers is necessary for survival. But there's a difference between having a crowd of spectators and having a real partnership with people who are invested

## BUILD RELATIONSHIPS THAT WORK

in your success. Those are the relationships that will remain when the cheering stops. Why? Because quality matters. Think about it. How often do you check the quality of the products and services you purchase? You do this to ensure they will meet, and will continue to meet your needs. There are no warranties or guarantees in relationships. It's trial and error, yet you must evaluate your relationships when necessary. Evaluation doesn't mean there's anything wrong; on the contrary, it's great to see how you can improve or expand your partnerships. Of course, there will be times when a relationship requires purging toxic behavior. You may consider to reevaluating them entirely if something happens to make you question why you came together in the first place. If talking through those moments aren't fruitful, it's is okay to part ways. Kicking the tires on relationships is a mental check to make sure the appeal continues by maintaining a standard of excellence in them. Relationships are mutually inclusive—meaning each party must be in agreement, working together by bringing individual strengths, talents, perspective and experiences to the table! There is **no** relationship without the contribution of everyone involved.

5. **Authenticity** is the best way to create strong partnerships. Being yourself and showing up confidently is a magnet for those who appreciate ingenuity. Confidence is contagious! When you are comfortable in your skin, you give others permission to be comfortable in theirs, and *that* is attractive. Maya Angelou said it best, *"I've learned that people will forget what you said, people will*

*forget what you did, but people will never forget how you made them feel."* When you show up genuine and strong in your values, it will change the aura of any space from chaotic to peaceful. Be sensitive to other's needs as well. Nurture relationships and appreciate the value others bring, not just the resources they spend on you. This kind of influence beckons others to work with you, partner with you and spend time with you. As you build relationships, consider a few more awareness and authenticity tips:

- Be aware of your emotions and those of others and maintain your composure in volatile situations. Never allow negative emotions to overrule your intelligence.

- If there's a problem, talk about it when it happens. Avoid stewing, marinating, keeping score or operating from a place of judgment while you're nursing your hurt feelings.

- Be respectful and empathetic to the needs of others. It's not necessary to agree, but it is necessary to be respectful. Honor their right to need what they need.

- Accept others for who they are, not who you want them to be. You can't change people, but you can influence them by the standards and boundaries you practice.

- Honor your word, follow up and follow through on your commitment. Excuses have no place in your authenticity practice. If you're wrong, confess immediately.

- Be consistent in your presence, message and values. Social platforms help to grow your audience, so make sure your presence there aligns with your belief system. Resist jumping on the bandwagon of popular yet contrary trends.

Nowadays, everything is so automated that the humanity of building relationships is often missing. I'm not knocking technology. What I *am* knocking is the disconnect that happens when everyone retreats to their private space behind the computer and tries to form meaningful relationships via the internet. People tend to say things in e-mail and on social media that they might not say in a face-to-face interaction. Be careful not to alienate partners this way. If you're in business, a leader and if you want to have good solid relationships, you must still operate as if you were looking into the eyes of your partner. Character. Integrity. Standards. They still apply. As you practice self-awareness and control over your emotions and behavior, you will have greater influence as you enter relationships. Operating in an emotionally mature state helps you attract the kinds of fulfilling relational environments where you can thrive. Isn't **that** what you want? Isn't that what you **need**?

**Recap and Challenge**

One more thing: Don't forget that you are enough, and you have everything you need, to achieve your goals. Just remember, you are not an island! Relationships are necessary for support, to lean into when life is difficult. They lift you when you stumble. Friends pray for you when you hurt and pour back into you when your energy is spent.

Build a tribe of people who stretch you and challenge your thinking. True friends are confident enough to speak up when you're wrong and are willing to tell you the truth, whether you like it or not. I challenge you to consider those closest to you and see how they show up in your life and make sure they have your best interest at heart. Surround yourself with people who are unwilling to sit idly by and watch you settle for less than you deserve. Your friends will cry with you, then tell you to get up and get back in the game. They will match the value you bring into the ring. See the possibility of powerful relationships and the differences you will make in the world…together.

# BUILD RELATIONSHIPS THAT WORK

SELF-APPROVED

## CHAPTER 8:

# For Every Milestone Achieved, Affirm and Celebrate

*"Celebrate what you've accomplished but raise the bar a little higher each time you succeed."*

—Mia Hamm

When your faith is shaken, frustration creeps in. When what you tried didn't work or when all hell is breaking loose, what you speak to yourself matters. Your words are the difference between giving in to pressure or using challenges as a springboard to bounce back. Why do I say this when what you want is positive and uplifting experiences? I want you to be savvy about reality and to be as prepared as possible when difficulties arise. I want you to know that challenges will come, no matter how hard you work and that things won't always work out according to plan. And it's okay. There is no growth without challenge and no testing of faith if everything is going well.

*"Awareness keeps you focused. Preparation keeps you ready. Confidence keeps you moving. And your mind and thought processes support them all."*

—Necie Black

## SELF-APPROVED

Let's talk about affirmations. Contrary to what you may believe, affirmations are not always positive. You can affirm anything, whether it's good or bad. How many times have you said, "It's a bad day," or "I'm always broke?" You are guaranteeing a bad day and that you will *always* be broke. I've heard people defend a very nasty attitude as if it's something to be proud of, affirming their ability to "go off" on you at the drop of a hat. Remove negative affirmations like, "Oh, that's just how I am." No, it's not. It's how you choose to be, and it limits your ability to grow past what you're defending. You can choose differently. You can decide to do better. When you want growth and change, reinforcing negative behavior with justifying words only serve to lower your self-esteem. There is so much power in the words you speak—power to build up or tear down—so change the words you say to yourself about your circumstances. You can speak lack or life. Choose to speak life, and give yourself constant reminders of how brilliant you are, even if you don't feel brilliant. Be your own inspiration so you can encourage yourself at any moment.

Inspiration and motivation come from many sources. Scroll through any social media platform and you find one, two or ten thousand images, filled with inspiration. It's fabulous to see so many quotes and funny clichés to lighten the mood. It's even more fabulous to have a personal system of resources you can draw inspiration from, created by you with **your** needs and goals in mind. While you can glean feel-good and warm fuzzies from others, look within and connect with your source of inspiration to create your own library of affirmations from which to draw inspiration.

## Make positive affirmation a lifestyle

Now that you've grown in confidence and stepped out of the box, it's necessary to maintain your momentum by learning how to speak to yourself about you and your goals. Your attitude will reflect what's going on in your head and heart, so re-train your brain to keep your thoughts uplifting, as well as what comes out of your mouth. Affirmations are a great way to organize the right words for any challenging situation. The goal is to accentuate your positives by rearranging the way you use specific words when speaking about negative circumstances. It can affect how you see the situation.

For example, when you use words like *me*, *my*, and *mine*, you are claiming ownership of whatever the words reference. So, if I say "my trouble," I take ownership of it. When I say **my** sickness, I *own* the sickness. The shift comes by replacing words like "my" with the word "the." It then becomes "the" trouble or "the" sickness. That way, the trouble or sickness is identified as a byproduct of circumstances you don't own. Sure, your body may feel the effects of an illness, but you surely don't want to claim ownership of it. I don't want to claim sickness and certainly want no part of trouble. Why would I? Why would you? Practicing positive thinking allows you to focus on your strengths and accomplishments, which increases happiness and motivation. Aligning your mind to believe, and your words to speak on what's good, prosperous, and forward moving, is the focus of positive affirmations.

Creating affirmations is a fun way to reinforce your confidence and lift yourself from a state of doubt and uncertainty. You can explore a variety of positive words by cross-referencing just one; bring them together to fit you. Here are a few tips to creating and utilizing personal affirmations:

1. Make your affirmations **Positive** and **Powerful**! They don't have to be long at all to be effective so 3-5 words will suffice. Here are a few examples: I Am Enough. I am Confident! I live in Abundance. Money flows to me easily. They are short, to the point and easy to remember. Your words will reflect how you see yourself, the value you bring and the results you want to create. Make sure your affirmations create positive impact.

2. Put your affirmations on **Paper**! Write them down in a journal or notebook and post them on sticky notes in visible locations around the home, office, car, refrigerator or on a mirror. Use these visual cues as a reminder to speak them to yourself. Memorizing them is great, and if you're a visual learner, visualizing them is even better. Place the most powerful ones in the areas you need them most. For example, if you work in a stressful or chaotic environment, use affirmations there that bring you comfort and peace.

3. Make your affirmations **Personal**! They are for and about you specifically. No one else. No family or friend's opinion of you counts, even if you agree with them. It's okay to use a friend's affirmations as a springboard into *your* deepest desires, but the ultimate statement must be your own choice of words. Too many people repeat affirmations they hear others speak because they sound good, but the affirmations may not be a true reflection of what you want. Creating your own affirmations

provides the space you need to choose self-care and concretes your commitment to them.

4. State your affirmations in **Present** tense. Let's say you are envisioning what you want a year, five or ten years from now. Snatch that vision out of the future and bring it into your present as if it is already happening. This is intentional. Affirm that you are what and who you desire to be right now. That means eliminating words like "will" and "going to be" and "want to" because they indicate what's to happen in the future. Remember the positive and powerful examples I used in step one? Here's how they show up by removing future references:

    - I am Enough—**Am** defines your state of being. You wouldn't say I "will be" enough or I want to be enough. Right?

    - I live in Abundance—**Live** defines what you occupy. You don't "want to" live in abundance. Right now, not down the road.

    - I have Peace—**Have** defines your possession of peace. You want peace, yes, but to say "I want peace" indicates you don't have it. Take possession and OWN your peace.

5. Be **Persistent** in viewing and speaking your affirmations every day. Take a few moments throughout the day to meditate on your affirmations and what they mean to you. Reaffirm your commitment to your success.

6. They are **Purposeful** in situations that you have no control over. When things don't go the way you want them,

your affirmations keep you grounded and focused on a *positive* outcome.

7. **Record** and **Playback** your affirmations often—there is nothing like hearing **your** voice remind you of how amazingly awesome you are. Most mobile devices have a recording feature on them that allows you to keep voice memos of your affirmation. Or use your video recorder and make a video. Both are great ways to keep affirmations available to you at all times. Let's face it, when are any of us without a mobile device? Even if you don't have service on it, the recording feature and the ability to save the file on the device still works. Allow your positive words to delve deeply into your subconscious mind and thrive in your spirit. When doubt or negativity arise, use affirmations to conquer them.

Using affirmations reinforces what you see as possible and allows you to speak to yourself differently. Positive words take the place of stagnant ones. As your faith grows, so will the strength of your affirmations. No matter what's going on around you, allow yourself the affirming power of self-validation. Based on what you just learned, take a few moments and write out **ten** affirmations that are Positive, Powerful, Personal, in Present tense and write them here:

_____

_____

_____

_____

# AFFIRM AND CELEBRATE

_____
_____
_____
_____
_____
_____
_____
_____
_____
_____

Take a good look at them and say each one out loud. Louder. LOUDER! Repeat them often, and don't forget to place them in areas where you can view and speak them. If you have a smart phone, record them and replay them in the morning when you arise, during the day, when trouble comes and before you go to sleep at night. Allow them to grow as you do, and incorporate new ones along the way. Allow personal and positive affirmations to become a way of life for you. They will become a lifestyle of documented tools you can reach for any moment you choose.

**Make it a point to toot your horn.**

A lot of times women shy away from the spotlight, opting to serve in the background. It's safe and comfortable back there, because performing at the level you're capable of isn't a challenge you're willing to accept. Maybe you feel as if you're boasting by positioning for the spotlight. Maybe you care that others believe you aren't being humble enough, when actually it's not about humility. It's about everyone having their moment in the spotlight. Could it be possible that you're not prepared for the influx of applause you'll receive as a result of stepping out of your comfort zone? You may be so accustomed to giving compliments to others that it's difficult to receive them for yourself. At some point in your life there will be a moment you must step into the light. Put your talents to greater use by getting out on the stage.

Know that every level of growth brings added responsibility and yes, you can handle it. Trust when greater demands it, you will always rise to the occasion. Besides, who's going to know what you can do unless you share? Get out there and let people see, applaud and celebrate with you. It's not just about positioning yourself in a space you'd like to be; it's about showing yourself that you *can* and *will* accomplish whatever you set your mind to do. Are you willing to test the limits on your capabilities? Show up ready and willing to do what's necessary to achieve your dreams. You've prepared. You've prayed. God's got you. You are ready and the world needs you to show up. You must to shine and I call forth the greatness in you. You are bold, strong and confident—and you're doing everything you wanted because YOU CAN!!

Begin within to accept, love and respect who you are. No matter what you've been through, you can always begin again. Remember, no one has it all together; we are **becoming**. There is always more. Greater. Higher. Farther. Re-imagine and see yourself through God's eyes. Believe you are worth love, hope, a future and second chances because the sacrifice of Jesus made it possible. Yes, you can live an authentic and purposeful life. I'll close with one of my favorite songs, "*I Am What You See*" led by Bishop Paul S. Morton, Sr.

> *Help me to see me*
> *The way you see me*
> *Sometimes I see pain Lord*
> *When you see victory*
> *I see where I am Lord*
> *You see where I shall be*
> *Open my eyes, help me believe*
> *I am what you see*
>
> *You see me victorious*
> *You see me faithful*
> *You see me believing*
> *That you are able*
> *You see me rejoicing*
> *That I have survived*
> *Open my eyes, help me believe*
> *I am what you see.*
>
> *I am healed*
> *I am free*
> *I am what you see.*
>
> *Open my eyes, help me believe*
>
> *I am what you see.*

# SELF-APPROVED

CHAPTER 9:

# Trust and Celebrate Your Progress

*"A bird sitting in a tree is never afraid of the branch breaking, because her trust is not on the branch but in the **strength** of her wings. Always believe in yourself."*

—Unknown

Ok, so I added the word *strength* because it wasn't a part of the original quote. My question is: what about her wings does this bird trust? Is it that she knows she's a bird and her wings were made for flying, that she's flown with them before so she knows how they will perform, or is it because she knows they are healthy and strong? It could very well be all three. Growth is a process that does not happen overnight, and bringing forth your dreams can be daunting. You must know who you are, and whose you are in faith and confidence. Trust that you are right where you need to be, doing what you should be doing. Trust the process that you've developed and the contributions you are making in your life. You've overcome so much to get where you are, so have faith in the strength of your wings. As you continue to affirm yourself, build confidence and show yourself some love, remember to:

- Be positive. Attitude is a little thing that makes a big difference.
- Surround yourself with happy and inspiring people.
- Remind yourself of everything you have to be grateful for.
- Always choose joy in your journey.
- Throw your arms around yourself and give yourself a hug.

I've heard before that the only thing in life that will always remain the same is change. You have the power to make any changes you desire. As you do, I challenge you to celebrate intentionally. Do something that rewards every forward step you make. Whether that means taking yourself to dinner and a movie, or soaking in a warm tub of bubbles, put it on your calendar and ***do*** you! Celebrate your progress because it represents movement from where you are to where you're going; from who you are to who you are becoming.

## AFFIRM AND CELEBRATE

SELF-APPROVED

# EPILOGUE:
# Rules of Engagement

Writing this book was a labor of love with a sincere desire to see you rise above challenge and mediocrity. Do you agree the goal is not just to read for inspiration, but to apply the lessons inside and create the change you want? Now that you've completed all chapters, let's revisit the key principles you've learned.

1. **Self-Esteem—The Confidence Gap**: It's not sexy to say, "I have low self-esteem" yet it may be evident in how you operate in life, work and/or relationships. You have the power to change the way your life looks and feels any time you choose. You want change? Tap into your power with authenticity; drop the façade and recognize how low self-esteem is showing up in your life. If necessary, revisit areas in your life that left you feeling as if you are unworthy or undeserving of a healthy, prosperous and fulfilling life. To start, you must intentionally take off the blinders and see yourself and circumstances objectively. Not from a place of judgment, but of improvement.

Start the process of building and reinforcing self-esteem by following a few simple rules:

- Denying you have an issue, is an issue. Be willing to face the truth of what's going on inside you. Consider your mental and emotional well-being and have open and honest dialogue with yourself about where you are, and where you really want to be.

- Believe that you deserve to be happy. It does not matter what your life has been like up to this point, it *can* change. Reject thoughts of inadequacy by not allowing yourself to wallow in past failures.

- Action is an intentional way to counter fear. Commit to removing the roadblocks that are holding you back from living a happier life; even if that roadblock is you.

2. **Self-Validation and Its Healing Ability**: Shared how to uproot seeds of insecurity planted in your mind and heart by negative people or experiences. Insecurity affects the attitude you carry throughout your life, and is directly related to how you see yourself in the world, how you show up, and whether you believe in who you are. A lack of confidence and self-esteem creates a cycle of self-degradation and prevents women from loving themselves wholly. This negative self-perception makes it challenging to thrive in a society where women are judge and accepted (or not) based on their physical appearance. The goal of this chapter is for each woman to heal from a negative past, and define their own standard of beauty by following a few rules of self-acceptance:

- Develop a positive attitude by exploring your body. Get to know and appreciate the strength and unique features you possess. Love who you are, just the way you are.

- If there is anything you want to change about your body, do it for you. To help you feel better. Don't change to live up to society's standard of what's beautiful. Physical appearance will never replace inner beauty—no matter what.

- Resist finding your worth in the applause of others, or sacrifice your dignity for the sake of being liked or accepted.

3. **The Process of Self-Assessment**: Introduced the ICMe3™ Principles of Self-assessment. The principles include thought-provoking questions to develop self-awareness, to control thoughts and behaviors, and identify ways to improve with intentional action. Sometimes you just don't know what you don't know, until you know it. While it takes time, and grace *getting to know you better*, the results are necessary to build confidence and esteem. Take the time to figure things out. To discover your inner and outer workings so you are not a mystery—to you!

   - Take inventory of all that you possess—your skills, gifts, thoughts, behaviors, insecurities, and even the flaws. Remember to tend your attitude and personality, if they need adjusting, and take notice of how you show up and represent yourself.

- Know what you want, need and expect out of life. Position yourself with the action necessary to create what you decide is in your best interest.

- Give yourself permission to be who you are, genuinely. Find value in what makes you different. Allow even your quirky personality to show through. Validate your goals and dreams as true to where you want to go.

- Don't judge yourself for past mistakes or dwell on what went wrong. Focus on the future and how you expect to live happier, healthier and exactly how you want to be.

4. **Allow Your Gifts Their Space** means to give your natural gifts, skill and talent the room they need to grow and flourish. Open yourself to opportunities to test the strength of all you can do. You won't discover the depth of your potential or the reach of your capabilities until you venture into territory outside of the familiar. Think about how alive you feel when you are in the zone of doing what you love and enjoy. Don't be afraid to draw upon the power of your talent.

    - Place a priority on developing your gifts. The more you put your talent to use, the stronger they become and the more fruitful your life will be—opening additional doors.

    - You have something special to share with the world. Someone has a problem and your life's gift will provide the solution.

EPILOGUE—RULES OF ENGAGEMENT

- As you allow your gift to bring joy, passion and purpose to your life, you cement your ability to become who God created.

5. **Subscribe to Self-care Therapy:** Not only is important to build the tenacity and strength physically to get through your day to day, your mind and spirit must be strong as well. Don't wait until you are too exhausted before you rest. Know your limitations and be aware of symptoms that could indicate something is going awry in your body. Taking care of yourself isn't just for the mind and body, it applies to the overall well-being of your life.

    - Keep your space negativity free by reinforcing personal boundaries. Surround yourself with people, places and things that makes you happy and allows you to be yourself.
    - Create healthy, sustainable habits so your body will function properly during times of stress, late nights, deadlines or emergencies.
    - Be okay using the power of **no,** especially when saying yes will over-extend and exhaust your resources.
    - Consistency is necessary. Make self-care non-negotiable. Schedule your *me* time if necessary, but make it a part of daily living.

6. **Turn Your Vision into Action**: Sit down and think carefully about what you want to do in life; what you want the future to look and feel like. What impact do you want your presence to create in the world? Your vision

is more than a compilation of wishes and dreams, it is your life's work. The thread that weaves your purpose into existence and you can't take it lightly. The process to create actionable steps should not just be Specific, Measurable, Agreed-upon, Relevant and Time-bound, you must connect to your goal in a way that support and sustains your passion along the way. Start by identifying the quality of your goal to include:

- Substance—Know what makes the goal important to you, as it will create the drive you need to push past challenges.

- Merit—See the value having completed this goal will bring. Is it worth investing time, energy and resources. Not just for you, but others?

- Authentic—The goal must be real for you. What you genuinely want and not something imparted to you another.

- Relevance—See the bigger picture of your life and make sure your goal fits into the overall scheme of your life. Does achieving this goal open the door for future ones?

- Tangible—Make sure goal is not too far out of reach that you are frustrated trying to attain it. Break it into smaller chunks so you will have something to celebrate along the way.

7. **Build Relationships That Work**: When you invite someone into your space, and vice-versa, there is a joint responsibility to create the kind of connection where

everyone thrives. Relationships are not one-sided, they are mutually inclusive of the unique value each party brings to the table. Everyone wins. If you desire quality in your relationships, start with these quick tips:

- Good relationships are built on honesty and trust. Relax and be yourself, be honest, be committed in bringing out your best and support the best in those around you.

- Not everyone sees things the same as you. People are individuals with their own unique thoughts and ideas. Allow others to be who they are, not who you want them to be.

- Communicate clearly. Recap and rephrase what you think you hear to mitigate misunderstandings. The goal is not just to be heard, but to hear with the intent to understand.

- Not every relationship is a good one for you. Test the motives and be diligent in protecting your space against negativity and fraud. Look for quality in relationships, instead of quantity.

8. **For Every Milestone Achieved, Affirm and Celebrate**: This is critical. The fact is, we all get frustrated and discouraged from time to time. Setbacks are temporary and does not mean the end of everything you want to accomplish. Have grace in your journey and commit to incorporating these quick tips into your day:

- Stay excited about your goals by celebrating every successful step you make. Be your own cheerleader and do something nice for yourself. Celebrating keeps you focused on the end goal, with a super-celebration when your goal is achieved.

- Make affirmations your lifestyle and the way you *do* living. Affirmations are self-esteem boosting, confidence building and sure-fire ways to maintain positivity and forward thinking.

- Take a moment to reflect on how far you've come. When you take time out regularly to inventory your gains, you're able to see what you've overcome to get where you are. That's tenacity and worth celebrating. #Grateful

# EPILOGUE—RULES OF ENGAGEMENT

# Necie Black
## RELATIONAL STRATEGIST

### Creating Synergy for Life and Business Relationships

Necie Black is a coach, speaker, consultant and trainer who shares leadership strategies for personal and professional growth. She inspires clients to align action in support of their dreams, purpose, and destiny. Born in Los Angeles, California on a crisp morning in December, Necie has a love for all things Christmas. As third eldest of eight children, she shared the responsibility of caring for her younger siblings and quickly learned to lead and resolve conflict. Necie excelled in school and in spite of becoming a teenage mom, she persevered to rise above life challenges. Necie spent over 27 years with a Fortune 500 Telecommunications Company and knows the importance of building strong relationships. As a Relational Strategist, she envisions an environment where employees are empowered to be creative and leverages their talent to increase productivity, efficiency and profitability. Working with leaders who are eager and committed to align their strengths with purposeful action, Necie is passionate to support them in bringing synergy to life and business relationships. As Founder of Lyfe Smarts LLC, Necie believes one of the stepping stones to success is continuous learning. Along with acquiring both Professional and Master Coach Certifications and Strengths Strategy Coaching Certification, Necie is a member of the International Coach Federation and holds a Bachelor's and Master's degree in Business Management from Amberton University, Garland, Texas. She volunteers and serves as Board of Directors Development Chair with Dress for Success, Oklahoma City, a non-profit organization providing a network of support, professional attire, and development tools to help women thrive in work and in life. Necie lives in the Oklahoma City area with husband Michael.

support@necieblack.com | 405-358-3510 | www.necieblack.com | @NecieBlack | f @lyfesmarts | @NecieBlack | @NecieBlack

## CONTACT
## NECIE

- @NecieBlack
- @lyfesmarts
- @NecieBlack
- @NecieBlack

405-358-3510
support@necieblack.com
**www.necieblack.com**

Creating Synergy for **Life** and **Business** Relationships

www.ingramcontent.com/pod-product-compliance
Lightning Source LLC
Chambersburg PA
CBHW070628300426
44113CB00010B/1703